T0266190

The Battle

The Battle

PLAYS, PROSE, POEMS
BY

Heiner Müller

✠—✠—✠—✠—✠—✠—✠—✠

Edited and Translated by Carl Weber

PAJ PUBLICATIONS
NEW YORK

For Marianne in gratitude

© 1989 Copyright by PAJ Publications
© 1989 Copyright of texts in the original held by Verlag der Autoren, Frankfurt, West Germany, representing Henschel Verlag, Berlin/DDR.
© 1989 Translation, preface, and introductory materials copyright by Carl Weber.

First Edition
All rights reserved
No part of this publication may be reproduced or transmitted in any form or by any means, electronic or mechanical, including photocopy, recording, or any information storage or retrieval system now known or to be invented, without permission in writing from the publishers, except by a reviewer who wishes to quote brief passages in connection with a review written for inclusion in a magazine, newspaper, or broadcast.

All rights reserved under the International and Pan-American Copyright Conventions. For information, write to PAJ Publications, 131 Varick Street, Suite 902, New York, N.Y. 10013.

Library of Congress Cataloging in Publication Data
The Battle
ISBN: 1-55554-048-1 (cloth)
ISBN: 1-55554-049-X (paper)

CAUTION: Professionals and amateurs are warned that the plays appearing herein are fully protected under the Copyright Laws of the United States and all other countries of the Copyright Union. All rights including professional, amateur, motion picture, recitation, lecturing, public readings, radio and television broadcasting, and the rights of translation into foreign languages, are strictly reserved. All inquiries concerning performance rights to texts appearing herein should be addressed to Elisabeth Marton, 96 Fifth Avenue, New York, N.Y. 10011.

Printed in the United States of America

Publication of this book has been made possible in part by grants received from the National Endowment for the Arts, Washington, D.C., a federal agency, and the New York State Council on the Arts.

The translation of *The Battle* was made possible, in part, by a grant from The Wheatland Foundation.

Contents

Preface

Carl Weber

THE YEAR THIS VOLUME is published, 1989, marks Heiner
Müller's sixtieth birthday. Born January 9, 1929, in Eppendorf,
Saxony—which today is in the southernmost part of the German
Democratic Republic—he began to write professionally thirty-nine
years ago and grew to become a critic, poet, playwright and, eventually, a stage director whose impact on the German theatre has
become as strong as it is controversial. In the last decade Müller has
been honored with the most prestigious literary prizes in both states
which emerged from the ruins of the German Reich after World War
II. There appears to be little disagreement regarding his importance
to literature and the theatre in the four German-speaking countries
of Central Europe: he is nearly unanimously acknowledged as the in-
heritor of Brecht's mantle, a writer who started in the old master's
footsteps but today is one of his outspoken critics. Refuting most of
Brecht's models, he proceeded to create his own paradigm of theatre.

The texts in this book trace Müller's development from the early years when he wholeheartedly embraced the views and the Epic theatre of Brecht to the period when he devised a radically different dramaturgy which was intended to present on stage the dizzying contradictions of twentieth-century history, as seen from the vantage point of its final decades.

REPORT ON GRANDFATHER is the earliest of Müller's writings that has been published, THE BATTLE marks the end of a period which had led him from experimentation with the Brechtian *Lehrstück* to the construction of his own theatrical model. The "synthetic fragment," as Müller named it, was one of the first experiments in European drama which responded to what might be called a "postmodern sensibility."

All the texts in the book, be they plays, narrative prose, or poetry grapple with issues history imposed on the German people in this century—conflicts which a majority failed to resolve or tried to avoid in determined efforts to protect their private realm, whether of family or of property. Müller offers in his first text for the theatre, THE SCAB, a realistic presentation of events and problems which, shortly after World War II, were encountered in the effort at building socialism in the eastern part of the former Reich, an effort which had to confront a people of former Nazis or Nazi sympathizers. The author soon moved on to explore the potential of poetic language for his topics, while modeling his dramaturgy as much after the classics as after Brecht's *Lehrstück*, illustrated by TRACTOR. Eventually he began to employ—in a kind of transference—parables derived from ancient mythology of the Western, i.e., Greco-Roman, tradition, which HERACLES 5 and THE HORATIAN demonstrate. These texts also explore further Brecht's dramaturgy of the *Lehrstück*. Müller's last and, as some feel, most powerful *Lehrstück* experiment was MAUSER, which constituted a radical critique of Brecht's model and ideology, as such a response to *The Measures Taken*, the most controversial text of Brecht's *Lehrstück* period. Müller's critique of the Brecht heritage continues in THE BATTLE, an answer to *Fear and Misery of the Third Reich*. THE BATTLE is a collection of short playlets about life in Nazi Germany, as Brecht's play was, yet it presents Müller's very different view of the German "collective mind" during Nazi rule, which Brecht misunderstood, according to Müller, since he was blindfolded by Marxist textbook ideology.

All these texts focus on crucial moments when individuals cannot escape the challenge history forces upon them and either face it or fail and perish in the confrontation. The texts also demonstrate Müller's continued discourse with Brecht's theatre, from the author's first performed and published play, THE SCAB, which emulates the Epic model Brecht had developed in his later years, through experiments which investigate and develop Brecht's *Lehstrück* dramaturgy of the early thirties; and finally, to Müller's critical response to *Fear and Misery of the Third Reich*, Brecht's effort at explaining by way of realistic representation the German mentality under Hitler's rule. Eventually, Müller turned Brecht's dramaturgy inside out and embraced the grotesque and Artaud's theatrical ideas in his work. In this context, TRACTOR is of interest: written in a mode of "heightened realism," combining verse with structural elements of the *Lehrstück*, it couldn't be published or performed in East Germany at the time of its completion. (As for the author's problems with GDR cultural policies, see my introduction to HAMLETMACHINE *and Other Texts for the Stage.*) On the occasion of the first printing of the play, in West Berlin, 1974, Müller inserted several pieces of poetry and prose into the text, an effort to turn it into a "synthetic fragment," his by then developed new dramaturgic model.

The previous two volumes of Müller's works (HAMLET-MACHINE and EXPLOSION OF A MEMORY) published by PAJ Publications, offered a comprehensive selection from Müller's writings during the last seventeen years. This book presents an overview of his work from 1950 to 1975. Though several full-length plays, such as THE FARMERS, THE CONSTRUCTION SITE, and WOMEN'S COMEDY aren't included, nor his adaptations of classic Greek tragedies, as OEDIPUS TYRANT, PHILOCTETES, and PROMETHEUS, the reader will find a wide variety of texts which encompass Müller's development from his earliest efforts as a writer to the mastery he had attained by the seventies when critics began to acclaim him as successor to Brecht.

The reader will discover certain threads which connect most, if not all, of Müller's thinking and writing. There is the conflict of the individual's desire for fulfillment, in other words: the pursuit of happiness, which clashes with the crushing demands history and its social upheavals force upon humankind. Müller has kept struggling with and writing about this conflict for forty years, from a perspective which might strike American readers as very European, if not sometimes Prussian.

The conviction that individuals are beholden to history and the social forces which are forged by it, is never forgotten by Müller. He may investigate and question the individual's commitment, he may discuss and distrust ideologies which enforce such a commitment, but he always maintains that the individual cannot escape a responsibility for humankind's present and future.

Underlying Müller's view of social responsibility is, of course, the insight that no person lives without being inextricably involved in, tied to, and fettered by the historical movement of humankind, regardless of an individual's ignorance, rejection, or acceptance of such a fact. In a period of American history when such an awareness is often deliberately suppressed, even laughed at, and when the consequences of such manipulated blindfolding of public awareness threaten to unravel the heretofore accepted social contract, Müller's quite opposite stance might be read as a healthy and sobering challenge.

The final text of the book is a discourse betwen Müller and the West German playwright and dramaturg Horst Laube. Much of their discussion deals with the theatre's and its author's responsibility in the society which supports their work. Their consensus about the theatre's social function, which is shared by their peers in the culture of their two countries, may sound remarkable, if not strange, to many American readers. It proposes a philosophy of theatre which still struggles to be accepted in this country, in spite of the many decades of effort and achievement in the American regional theatre movement. Commitment to society and commitment to a vital theate is inseparable in Müller's mind, as it certainly must have been to Shakespeare, if he ever reflected on the problem. Of all the contemporary Western playwrights, Müller may come closest to the Shakespearean stance which views history and theatre as two sides of the same coin.

* * *

I'd like to thank Dr. Karlheinz Braun of Verlag der Autoren, Frankfurt, for his support and encouragement of this project, and

Bonnie Marranca and Gautam Dasgupta of PAJ Publications for their firm belief in Heiner Müller's work and their help in putting together this book.

IMAGES

IMAGES (*Bilder*) was written in 1955. It was first printed in *Heiner Müller Geschichten aus der Produktion 2*, Rotbuch 126, Berlin 1974, the second volume of the collected edition published by Rotbuch Verlag, West Berlin.

The poem reads like a motto of Müller's work during the twenty-five years covered by the selections in this volume, a motto comprising the author's experience and anticipating his progress through the next decades.

C. W.

Images mean everything at the start. Are durable. Spacious.
But the dreams curdle, they take on a shape and frustration.
No image contains the sky any longer. The cloud from the
    airplane's
Angle: a vapor obstructing the sight. The crane just
    a bird.
Communism even, the ultimate image, always refreshed
Since washed with blood again and again, daily routine
Pays it out in small change, without sparkle, tarnished
    from sweat

The great poems: rubble, like bodies loved a long time and now
Of no use, at the wayside of a species that's finite but using up
    plenty

Between the lines: lamentation

                on the bones of the stone carriers: happy

Since the beautiful means the possible end of the horrors.

1955

REPORT ON GRANDFATHER

REPORT ON GRANDFATHER (*Bericht vom Grossvater*) was written in 1950. It was first published in the playbill for the production of *Die Umsiedlerin oder das Leben auf dem Lande*, at the Student Theatre of the College of Economy, Berlin Karlshorst 1961 (the production was cancelled by the East Berlin authorities after one performance). Thirteen years later, when Rotbuch Verlag began to publish its edition of collected works by Müller, the text became the opening piece of the first volume, *Geschichten aus der Produktion 1,* Rotbuch 108, West Berlin, 1974.

The short story is one of the first literary texts the author appears to have put to paper, and it still remains one of the very few published examples of his early prose. In subsequent years he began working on texts for the stage, but it wasn't until THE SCAB was published in 1957 that Müller, a young journalist, literary critic, and author of some poetic texts, was noticed as a dramatic talent.

In his report on the grandfather, Müller encapsulates the history of a large percentage of German working class people during the first half of the century, people whose attitudes contributed to the failure of the German revolution of 1918, to the rise and short-lived triumph of Hitler and, ultimately, to the disappearance of the Germany they grew up in. They were people left behind by historical developments which they failed to comprehend even as the political and social landscape of Europe kept rapidly changing throughout their lives. The text also demonstrates important roots from which Müller's writing has grown, and which still continue to nourish it.

C. W.

In July nights when gravity is weak
And his graveyard overflows its walls
The dead cobbler comes to visit me
The grandfather, the much beaten old man

My grandfather died when I was seventeen. My mother said of him: he was never ill, but his brains weren't quite right anymore at the end. Today, five years later, I know what wasn't right there.

His father died early. For the funeral of the dead bread-winner—the place beneath the ground doesn't come free—a cabinet had to be sold, an heirloom. The mother, alone with the child, spent a decade at the sewing machine, in poor light sewing shirts, so by the tenth year she at first couldn't see the eye of the needle, then the half-finished shirt and, finally, not even the light. The doctor recommended an operation but didn't bring along the money for it. So the operation couldn't be done. My grandfather took care of the blind woman, as of a child, until his fourteenth year. Then she died.

During his apprenticeship with a shoemaker he worked for a pittance, suffered hunger which he was used to, and was beaten: his master, turned into stone by an apprenticeship of a similar kind, handed down his experience. The beaten boy learned how to put up with the beatings, at best how to beat also, but not how to beat in the right direction. He wasn't a capable person. He didn't even become a master since you had to pay for the examination. He became a worker in a shoe factory.

Twenty years old, he married. His wife was the daughter of a rich farmer, yet she didn't bring any dowry since the farmer was against the marriage beneath her class. He who had learned early the art of hunger was a good instructor for his wife, and she learned well. They had ten children. Two died early, eight they could bring up. My mother, when conversation turns to her childhood, likes to use the parable of the salt herring. It's hanging at a long string way down from the ceiling. It always has to last for a week. Only on pay day is it renewed. Three times a day the procession of eaters—''one bite for each one''—marches by.

After the shoe factory went bankrupt during World War I, my grandfather found work with a bridge construction company. After an accident at work, a fall from the scaffolding onto the stony, nearly parched river bed, he was fired. Three more workers fell from the same scaffolding, one after another. Two were fired, the third one died on the spot. The two went to sue: the construction company had saved too much wood on the scaffoldings and was sentenced to pay. As for the dead man, he was shown to have been negligent. My grandfather, invited also to sue, said: I don't want trouble. Even twenty years after the accident his back pain increased when the weather changed. He then used to say: there is a good side to everything. For him, everything had its good side. Forced to eat dry bread, you learned to appreciate it; out of work you had time to go for mushrooms in the forest; doing piece work, you had no time for thoughts which only made you restless; when there was war, everybody had less. (Those tables which were more richly laid weren't shown to him, he wouldn't have seen them anyway, even had they been shown to him.)

He was on friendly terms with his ''betters.'' Better—that meant: not a worker. The employers of the town, all of them popular, liked to show themselves in the streets talking to the common people, especially to the elder ones.

During the troubled times after 1918 when in Saxony the workers were also fighting for a better life, he repaired the shoes of those on strike as well as those of the scabs, of the traitors along with the fighters, cheaper than anyone else. His shop was a corner of the kitchen. At that time he also started to go along to church when his wife asked him to, though he didn't care for it.

After the children were on their own, he drank on Saturdays. It was cheap for him since he couldn't tolerate it.

He wasn't for Hitler. When it became dangerous not to be for Hitler, he said if something went against his grain: Hitler doesn't know it; and when my father went to jail the second time because he couldn't put up with the new order: why didn't he shut up, one has to shut up, that's what they demand. I still remember that I, eight years old, one day on my vacation with him, hammered a good dozen nails into the floor. When my grandfather came in, he pulled them out, tried to hammer them straight again but didn't say a word. At that time iron was in demand again for the bigger flying nails, meant to strike through living hide, not the tanned one; plain nails were scarce.

After World War II, during the first months of hardship, the inconceivable happened; my grandfather, all his life a patient beast of burden, lost his patience as his life ran out. His wife's letters to my mother voiced the fear of God who might punish the man. She wrote that he was sinning against Him. She renounced him so that she wouldn't be punished with him. There was nothing contemptible in this: to her hell was real. My mother's siblings thought the incident was rather funny. The oldest one wrote: Father—it has to be said— isn't quite together anymore. Therefore he thinks only of himself. As if he is alone in this world. For instance, he took it into his head that he wants butter. But when butter was available, he only ate margarine. It's ludicrous. He's like a child. He simply doesn't believe her that she can't get butter for her money, he says she doesn't want to, she's stingy, she begrudges him everything. Mother suffers from it. He scolds her, he never used to do that. And formerly he was so modest.

I always was a good worker, he often said at that time, so I ought to be well-off today, in the worker's state. He didn't understand that patience was needed to eliminate the consequences of patience. Too many had endured too much for too long a time.

I still see him with his crinkled child's face, mindlessly content, later when his time was running out hardening into the sullen grimace of a clown who's taken off his make-up, him, my grandfather, a worker from Saxony, seventy-five years old, who died in 1946—impatient—of the consequences of patience.

THE SCAB

THE SCAB is a term which merely approximates the German title *Der Lohndrücker*, an East German idiom signifying a worker who lowers wage levels by establishing higher norms for a particular job.

The play was written in 1956, in collaboration with the author's first wife, Inge Müller, who had been a factory worker and contributed her own experience of the plant milieu, its language and social stratification. The text was first published in the East German literary magazine *Neue Deutsche Literatur,* # 5, 1957; it was later included in several anthologies and appeared in the first volume of the collected edition of Rotbuch Verlag, *Rotbuch 108,* 1974. The first performance, directed by Gunter Schwarzlose, opened March 23, 1958 at the Studio of Städtisches Theater Leipzig; it was presented September 2, 1958, together with THE CORRECTION (second version), at East Berlin's Maxim Gorki Theater in Hans Dieter Mäde's production. There was an important revival staged by Frank-Patrick Steckel at West Berlin's Schaubühne in the 1974-75 season.

Heiner Müller himself directed a production which opened at the Deutsches Theater, East Berlin January 28, 1988, where he radically deconstructed his text. Each part of the two-act performance opened with a brief film; the full text of THE HORATIAN was inserted at the beginning of Scene 1; *Centaurs*, Part 4 of VOLOKOLAMSK HIGHWAY, was presented as a nightmare of the Party Secretary in Scene 14 which concluded the performance.

The plot of THE SCAB is based on events which happened during 1948-49 at an East Berlin plant, VEB Siemens-Plania, where the bricklayer Hans Garbe pioneered the repair of furnaces while in operation—as described in the play—against the embittered resistance of most of his fellow workers. His successfully completed effort saved the factory half a million Marks; he consequently was rewarded with the honorary title ''Held der Arbeit'' (Hero of Labor) and eventually ended at a desk job in government, though the party organization in his plant had regarded him as a loner, a dreamer who regarded his job ''like a sport'' and showed ''ideological weakness.''

Garbe's story didn't only attract Müller. The East German writer

Eduard Claudius, for one, published a 1951 novel, *Men at Our Side*, which was based on the events at Siemens-Plania, and there were other literary treatments of Garbe's achievement. Brecht struggled with the material for several years but never got beyond a rough scenario and some scene sketches, known as the "Buesching fragment." He had been fascinated by Garbe/"Buesching's" past under Hitler and the obvious "gap between action and knowledge" which appeared to demonstrate the dialectics of history within one particular person. Müller widened this view and unfolds the contradictions within a group of protagonists, including his hero Garbe/"Balke," but ranging from the plant's director and its party secretary to the most lowly apprentice. The fable he constructed is, of course, largely fictional and doesn't aim at a documentation of Garbe's history. Among other aspects, the text presents an early example of Müller's fascination with the topic of "treason."

The play adapted, or rather, reshaped, models established by Brecht's work and also by the agit-prop theatre of the early thirties. It fitted a genre favored by official cultural policies in the GDR during the fifties, namely the so-called "production play"; these were texts which tried to motivate the population to increase their efforts towards improvement of production and living standards. While such plays were usually affirmative, positing worker-heroes against equally clear-cut class enemies, Müller's approach was far more critical, offering contradictory characters caught in, and torn by, the struggle "between the old and the new."

Reading the text, it is important to remember that by early 1948 all banks and companies owned by former Nazis or war criminals had been nationalized in East Germany; 8% of all industrial enterprises, responsible for 34% of total production, had become "People Owned Enterprises,": VEB. The government also had established a national marketing organization, HO ("Handels Organisation") which in those years sold goods and foodstuffs without the otherwise required ration coupons, but at steeply higher prices.

Finally, the newly established GDR began post-war reconstruction and the evolution of a Socialist society with a populace which had largely supported Hitler and willingly served the Nazi system.

C. W.

Helga Kneidl

THE SCAB
Schaubühne, Berlin, 1974. Director: Frank Patrick Steckel.
Scene 2.

Sibylle Bergemann

THE SCAB
Deutsches Theater, East Berlin, 1988. Director: Heiner Müller.
Scene 14.

The play doesn't try to present the struggle between the Old and the New—which can't be decided by a playwright—as concluded with the victory of the New before the last curtain. It tries to carry the struggle into the new audience who will decide it. The play takes place in the GDR, 1948/49. The history of the circular furnace is well known. The characters and their stories are invented.

H. M.

1

(Tavern. Street with a wall in ruins. Evening. The Innkeeper stands behind the bar drinking. Geschke and Stettiner drink, leaning against the bar. The Privy Councilor sits at a table. The street is empty.)

GESCHKE: *(Drunk.)* I've seen it all: the unemployment lines after the first war, piecework and the Nazis with trumpets and drums and, after the final mess, the new life with its bonus system. But the beer this workers' state is brewing is new to me. *(Stettiner laughs.)*

INNKEEPER: Workers' state. Workers' beer. *(Privy Councilor snickers.)*

GESCHKE: *(To the Innkeeper:)* Who's the scarecrow?

INNKEEPER: That's the Privy Councilor.

GESCHKE: A beer for the Privy Councilor. *(Innkeeper brings him the beer. Geschke lifts his glass.)* Drink, Privy Councilor. *(Privy Councilor refuses the beer and examines Geschke.)* A well-bred man, the Privy Councilor. Doesn't drink workers' beer. *(Pause. Then to Stettiner.)* Balke, the new guy who never opens his trap, has pocketed a bonus for his invention with the moulding. The invention works, you get done more.

STETTINER: Question is: For whom?

GESCHKE: (*Finishes his drink.*) We have to get out of this mess. What's that supposed to mean: for whom. You'll pay another round?

STETTINER: Do you actually believe what's written at the plant gate, "People's Property," eh? You're not that stupid, Geschke. You, too, are a worker, aren't you.

GESCHKE: Anyway, the boss is gone.

STETTINER: Go and buy yourself something with that. Another beer?

GESCHKE: (*Throws money on the bar, touches his cap and leaves, uncertainly.*) Question is: who's stupid around here.

STETTINER: The check. (*He steps into the street.*) Cigarette, Geschke? (*Geschke has crossed the street, stops, turns. Stettiner holds out a cigarette.*) Come here.

GESCHKE: All the way for one cigarette? No. (*Grinning, Stettiner lights another cigarette.*) Halfway. Alright? (*Stettiner grins. Geschke takes three steps in his direction, stops. Stettiner smokes.*) I'd do two steps more. (*He does so. Pause.*) Have a heart, Stettiner.

STETTINER: Two cigarettes.

GESCHKE: I said: Halfway.

STETTINER: Two cigarettes.

(*Pause. Stettiner throws a cigarette at Geschke's feet and leaves. Geschke picks up the cigarette, puts it in his pocket and leaves too. The Innkeeper has watched it all and laughing resumes his place behind the bar. On the street, a billposter appears and puts up a poster on the ruined wall; it reads: "SED—The Party of Reconstruction." When he is gone, a young man comes by, stops in front of the poster, looks around, rips it off, and walks on, whistling. Three workers, tired, carrying briefcases, walk across the poster on the ground.*)

2

(*Mess hall at the plant. Lunch hour. In the back wall there is a window where food is handed out in tin bowls. Stage right, an HO booth with a cardboard sign reading: "Onwards to new achievements!" The workers sit on wooden boxes and chairs at crude tables, spooning their soup, or they stand in front of the HO booth. The saleswoman arranges the merchandise, attaches price labels [Butter:*

"DM 60.00 a kilogram." Et cetera.])

STETTINER: Here's everything you need, Geschke. Buy.

GESCHKE: (*Scratching the bottom of his food bowl.*) The HO won't have change for my money.

A YOUNG WORKER: Are you selling butter by the gram, Miss?

SALESWOMAN: First grow up before you try kidding me, kiddy.

(*A bespectacled man, shortsighted, scrutinizes the price labels, while crouching and spooning his food.*)

STETTINER: Step up, ladies and gentlemen. Here's where you're skinned alive.

AN OLD WORKER: You shut up, Stettiner. You've shouted "Heil" loud enough. Now you can join us spooning up the mess you've helped to cook.

STETTINER: (*Grinning.*) It was Hitler who made these prices, right?

OLD WORKER: Right.

STETTINER: And he also made it cheaper for the West.

OLD WORKER: That remains to be seen.

SALESWOMAN: (*Since nobody is buying.*) Don't push. Everyone will be served.

KARRAS: What are you waiting for? (*He grabs a bottle of liquor, opens it, drinks; to Balke.*) Cheers, model worker! (*Balke is silent. Karras hands the bottle on to Zemke, he to Geschke, etc.*)

SALESWOMAN: (*To Karras, loudly.*) That's 41 Marks, colleague.

KARRAS: (*Reaches for the bottle.*) How's that?

GESCHKE: (*Wiping his lips.*) It's people's property, isn't it. Don't you read the paper, madame?

ZEMKE: You've been a member of the Nazi women's corps too long.

SALESWOMAN: (*To Karras.*) You haven't paid yet, Sir.

KARRAS: (*Finishes the bottle.*) I'll return the bottle. Alright?

SALESWOMAN: (*Loudly.*) Where's security?

KARRAS: (*To his fellow drinkers.*) Shall we share it? (*Silence. The bespectacled man leaves the mess hall.*)

A WORKER: Why do you booze, Karras?

KARRAS: 'Cause I have nothing to eat.

WORKER: Buy something.

KARRAS: And who's going to pay for the booze? (*He steps to the kiosk and pays.*) The receipt!

SALESWOMAN: How's that?

KARRAS: As a souvenir of 41 Marks.

SALESWOMAN: Don't have any receipts.

KARRAS: (*Tears a piece off the cardboard sign.*) There!

SALESWOMAN: (*Writes a receipt on the piece of cardboard.*) As you wish. (*Karras puts the piece of cardboard in his pocket and sits on a box, some distance from the others.*)

A VERY OLD WORKER: (*Staring at the price labels.*) The Nazis' necks have been broken. I thought: now it's going to begin, the new life we've risked everything for, and there'll be paradise for us workers.

ANOTHER ONE: The Soviet paradise.

VERY OLD WORKER: (*To Schurek:*) Now, I'm asking you: who can afford butter for 60 Marks?

BALKE: (*Steps to the booth.*) One pound of butter. (*Balke pays, the Saleswoman hands him the butter.*)

STETTINER: Not everyone has that kind of money.

GESCHKE: And not everyone is getting a bonus.

ZEMKE: Wash your hands, Miss, that money stinks.

STETTINER: There once was a man who got burned by a bonus.

SCHUREK: (*By rote.*) If we want to live better, we need to increase production. That's obvious, colleagues.

A WORKER: Let's ride to the vet, said the horse trader. But the nag had broken her leg.

STETTINER: Just like old times. The worker is the sucker.

BALKE: Don't crack your skulls, better use your heads.

ZEMKE: (*Trying to agitate.*) So what! If we tear this place apart, they'll put up a new one tomorrow!

BALKE: We've got to make the butter cheaper.

ZEMKE: Listen to the model worker.

KARRAS: And how is he going to do that, the smartass?

BALKE: (*Vehemently.*) Working better. (*Enormous laughter. Enter Engineer Kant. He walks up to Bittner who still sits and eats.*)

KANT: Three lids have cracked in Furnace Four, Bittner. They'll have to be repaired in three days or we'll be stuck.

BITTNER: (*Chewing.*) I know. But I've two bricklayers less than last week and no better material.

BALKE: We're six. Two men for one lid.

BITTNER: We work in threes, like always. We need three days for one lid. That's the norm.

BALKE: Fine, I'll take the second lid and set a new norm.

(*Pause.*)

LERKA: If they pay a bonus, I'll do the third one.

KANT: Alright.

BALKE: But we need handymen.

GESCHKE: What's a handyman getting?

ZEMKE: A stiff back.

BALKE: (*To Geschke.*) You'll do it?

GESCHKE: Not for free.

BALKE: We all work for money. Who'll make the handyman for Lerka? (*A bespectacled man who has come back stuffs a bite of bread into his mouth, steps forward, and lifts one finger.*)

LERKA: Fine.

GESCHKE: What's the handyman getting?

BITTNER: We'll lay bricks the way we're used to, old style and solid. You think you're super smart, Balke. When the lid you've repaired has cracked again, you'll think of me.

3

(*Factory hall. Workers, standing, or sitting, at breakfast or at cards.*)

DIRECTOR: Colleagues, so we'll proceed now to elect the union chair of our plant . . .

A WORKER PLAYING CARDS: I don't need one.

A WORKER EATING: Anyway, where is the old chair? Where's Kohn?

ANOTHER ONE: Where's the party secretary?

KARRAS: In the West. Kohn inherited a piece of land, and the party secretary went along to help digging. (*Laughter.*)

DIRECTOR: Schurek has been nominated. Of course, you can propose other nominations. You should know who you'd like to put your trust in.

A WORKER: Trust is well put.

ANOTHER ONE: If you trust you'll get bust. (*Laughter.*)

SCHUREK: Colleagues, we all know what's important. A clean record, a heart that beats for the colleagues, and loyalty to the workers' government—

(*Karras laughs.*)

DIRECTOR: Are you willing to accept, Schurek? (*Schurek nods bashfully.*) Well, I nominate our colleague Schurek, you all know him, and he knows his way around here. Do you have other proposals?

ZEMKE: Schurek kisses ass. (*Exits.*)

DIRECTOR: Are you making a proposal, colleague?

GESCHKE: (*To Stettiner:*) Whoever votes for Schurek can blame himself.

STETTINER: Are you willing to do the job? (*Geschke is silent.*) We'll never get justice. Not here. Who cares who'll be the bigwig.

ANOTHER ONE: We can't do a thing.

DIRECTOR: Well, whoever's for Schurek raise his hand.

(*The workers, including those who are still eating or playing cards, including Geschke, raise their hand, some holding a sandwich or playing card. Only a few exceptions, among them Karras.*)

KARRAS: I can't right now, my hand is in my pocket.

(*Director counts the votes.*)

4

(*Factory hall with furnace. Balke and Lerka at work on the furnace chamber lids. Geschke, Balke's handyman, and the bespectacled man, Lerka's handyman, are hauling bricks. Balke and Geschke construct from bricks and boards a bench around the chamber lid, place on it bricks, fire clay, mortar, and four lime troughs, one at each corner. Lerka is already laying bricks, very fast and sweating profusely; bricks, etc., but only one lime trough on the ground so that he needs to stoop for every single brick.*)

BALKE: You'll kill yourself that way. Get four lime troughs, and put all your stuff on the bench.

LERKA: Yeah, and put all the work off!

BALKE: You'll save it later.

LERKA: Each minute cost me ten pennies.

BALKE: You'll kill yourself.

LERKA: (*Groaning.*) Better one year less but a better life. (*Balke works, Lerka keeps toiling. Geschke and the Bespectacled Man, their handymen, arrive with empty backpacks, without bricks. Lerka to Bespectacled Man.*) More bricks!

SPECTACLES: The bricks are all gone.

GESCHKE: (*To Balke.*) What's left is wet.

LERKA: (*To Bespectacled Man.*) Bring me what you can get.

SPECTACLES: And what if the lid's going to crack?

LERKA: Get bricks. (*Bespectacled Man exits.*)

BALKE: (*To Geschke.*) Ask the engineer where we get dry bricks. (*Geschke exits. Pause.*) Lerka, do you know what you're doing when you're laying wet bricks? (*Bespectacled Man brings wet bricks, Lerka lays bricks.*)

LERKA: Speed or quality work. They can't have everything.

BALKE: The minute costs ten pennies, Lerka. But the furnace costs more.

LERKA: (*Nervous.*) Who's going to make me accountable? This place here is people's property, right? I am the people, you know. (*Balke is silent.*)

5

(*Accountant's office. Office of the Director. A narrow hallway in between. The Director enters the office in his overcoat. He takes the coat off, sits at his desk. The Accountant walks across the hallway into the director's office. Miss Matz, alone in the accountant's office, interrupts her work on payrolls and works instead on her finger-nails.*)

ACCOUNTANT: I'd only like to tell you, Sir, this won't work. A schedule that's based on the assumption that the furnaces are always working at capacity is irresponsible, with the shape our furnaces are in. One failure and we'll face chaos!

DIRECTOR: (*Looking at his two-day stubble in the piece of a broken mirror, not very attentive.*) We're facing chaos, Mister. We're reconstructing a devastated country. That spells: manufacture, manufacture at any price.

ACCOUNTANT: Maybe production will be the price. I'd only like to have pointed that out. I'm washing my hands of it. (*He walks back into the accountant's office. Miss Matz is putting on make-*

up.) You're at your make-up again, Miss Matz.

MISS MATZ: Is it my fault that the lipstick is crap?

(*Pause. The Director takes off his jacket and puts out his shaving things.*)

ACCOUNTANT: Formerly, you kept your schedules but you didn't throw out the baby with the bathwater. There was a profit. Foreign countries were interested in our product, and the workman had enough to eat. That was exploitation. Nowadays, we've been liberated of that.

MISS MATZ: Very funny.

ACCOUNTANT: (*Snaps.*) Are the payrolls ready, Miss Matz? (*Miss Matz is silent, works intensively. The Director begins to lather his face. The soap won't foam. Schurek appears in the hallway, behind him Geschke.*)

GESCHKE: Listen, Schurek, I need them. Am I supposed to work in my bare feet? (*He shows him a pair of worn out shoes.*)

SCHUREK: All our rations have been allotted.

GESCHKE: I was passed over again.

SCHUREK: We're making clay containers, fire-bricks for industry, and so forth, we don't make shoes, we don't print ration cards. I can't break all the rules for your sake. We've got to make sacrifices for Socialism.

GESCHKE: So I'm supposed to march barefoot towards Socialism, right? You're a scream, Schurek. (*Schurek leaves Geschke standing in the hallway and enters the Director's office. Geschke looks at his shoes. A young man, the Journalist, arrives, he enters the office. Exit Geschke.*)

DIRECTOR: (*Still lathering his face, to the Journalist he had expected.*) You're the newspaper man?

JOURNALIST: I need something on production achievements for the Sunday magazine.

DIRECTOR: That will be tough.

JOURNALIST: How are we doing with Socialist working contests?

DIRECTOR: No boot walks by itself alone.

JOURNALIST: What's that?

DIRECTOR: First somebody's got to put it on the foot.

JOURNALIST: (*Taking notes.*) I see. Rearguard leadership.

DIRECTOR: (*Angry.*) You're obstructing production, Sir!

JOURNALIST: (*Grins.*) Production of foam, I guess?

DIRECTOR: If our soap would make half as much foam as our newspaper people do.

SCHUREK: (*To the Journalist.*) I've got something for you, Colleague. Socialist contest. Wait here, I'll get the engineer. (*He exits. Silence in Director's and Accountant's office. The Director is shaving. Schurek comes back with engineer Kant.*)

KANT: (*To the Journalist.*) Kant.

JOURNALIST: Of the great philosopher's family, I assume? (*He laughs excessively.*)

KANT: Not really.

JOURNALIST: You're working with innovative Soviet methods, Socialist contests?

KANT: Do you know what a circular furnace is?

JOURNALIST: (*By rote.*) A furnace with firing chambers in a circular lay-out which serve sequentially as pre-heating, drying, baking, and cooling chambers, for burning of cement, clay, firebricks, etc., without interruption. Capacity of a chamber: 24 cubic feet, lids and walls made of fire-clay, temperature 1000 degrees Celsius. Hot work.

DIRECTOR: Maybe he knows all the encyclopedia by rote?

KANT: We're short of furnaces, after the bombing raids. We have to close down if one of them isn't operative. Materials aren't much anymore. Three lids in one furnace have recently cracked, a week after we've lost two bricklayers; one of them went to a sanitarium, the other one across the border. We had three days to repair them.

JOURNALIST: Sabotage, right?

KANT: I told you already: materials are poor.

SCHUREK: You said: not much.

JOURNALIST: I see. Objective obstacles.

KANT: The foreman, an old specialist, explains: it is impossible to do the job in three days. Correct is: the norm allows three days for one lid.

JOURNALIST: ''A specialist will never kill himself./If the roof falls in, he hides under a shelf.'' One of mine.

KANT: Two not so old specialists have set a new norm. That's all.

JOURNALIST: Fabulous.

(*Enter Lerka, his face bloody and scratched. He stops inside the door.*)

LERKA: (*To Kant.*) The lid is gone.

(*Pause.*)

SCHUREK: You laid the bricks, Lerka.

KANT: You've used wet bricks, right?

LERKA: Not really, Engineer, Sir, I always was a good worker, but if you're asked to work faster than you should. Ten hour workdays and for breakfast nothing but stale bread, and four kids and a sick wife.

KANT: Do you know what you've done, Lerka?

LERKA: Will you take it out of my pay? Forget the bonus, I'm aware of that.

SCHUREK: That's sabotage. You'll pay for that.

DIRECTOR: Anyone hurt?

LERKA: No.

KANT: You're bleeding.

LERKA: (*Wipes blood off his face with the back of his hand.*) A scratch. (*Kant exits, the Journalist after him. As Lerka moves to follow, the Director addresses him.*)

DIRECTOR: Lerka, I don't know why you've done that. But I can't pretend you didn't do it. I'm not sitting here for my own sake or for the fun of it.

LERKA: You can't bite my head off for a mistake. Do you think I wanted the lid to crack.

SCHUREK: You've cut into your own flesh. Now, don't scream it's hurting.

(*Pause.*)

LERKA: So that's the way it is. You slave till you're a cripple, thirty years you're kicked in the back, you eat like a dog and run like a nag. And now the word is: saboteur! So that's what your workers' state is like. You ain't better than the Nazis.

DIRECTOR: (*In a choked voice.*) Say that again.

LERKA: I said, you ain't better than the Nazis. (*The Director hits Lerka in the face. Pause.*) That'll cost you your job, Director. This isn't like with Hitler. (*He exits. Pause. Then, the Director*

walks across the hall into the Accountant's office.)
DIRECTOR: Are the payrolls ready?
MISS MATZ: Yes.

6a

(*Accountant's and Director's office. The Director at his desk reading, listlessly and with obvious effort. In front of him a stack of books on accounting. The Accountant is paying out wages, to Geschke, to the Bespectacled Man, to Balke.*)

ACCOUNTANT: (*To Balke.*) I've been told to pay you 400 percent. So you're getting Mr. Lerka's money too?
BALKE: Yes, 400. According to the old norm. I have to insist on it. Or we won't get the new norm we need. If you make it hard for them, they'll take it easy. (*Geschke and the Bespectacled Man look on as Balke pockets the money. They walk into the Director's office, Balke exits.*)
GESCHKE: The model worker is getting a bonus. We hauled the bricks. (*The Bespectacled Man nods.*)
DIRECTOR: Everybody can do what you did.
GESCHKE: I won't do it again. (*Exits with Bespectacled Man. Schurek enters the office, waving a newspaper.*)
DIRECTOR: (*Nervous.*) What do you want?
SCHUREK: (*Picks up a book and reads the title: "Double Entry Accounting."*) Will the accountant be fired?
DIRECTOR: No, but controlled. What do you want?
SCHUREK: (*Opens the paper where Balke's picture is.*) Here. The best horse in our stable. That'll be pinned on the blackboard. (*He tears off the page with the picture, takes thumbtacks from his pocket, pins the page on the wall, steps back, and checks the effect.*)
DIRECTOR: This here is no stable. (*Goes on reading. Schurek exits. The newspaper picture remains pinned on the wall. The Director takes a bottle and shot glass from his desk, drinks. Enter Schorn, the new party secretary of the plant. The Director, after an attempt to hide glass and bottle, puts a second glass in front of Schorn.*)
SCHORN: (*Pushes the glass aside.*) Thanks.
DIRECTOR: (*Fills his glass.*) We're in the hot seat here. You won't

have it easy as party secretary. You're the third one. (*He drinks.*) The first was wiped out by booze. He started to drink because of sabotage. The second was a greenhorn, straight out of party school, a pencil pusher. He's in the West now. The workers have no confidence in the party. Fascism is still in their bones. Once, they turned shells with their hands and feet, today they scream: "Piecework is murder!" If you ask me: I don't trust anyone. (*He drinks.*)

SCHORN: (*Points at the newspaper page.*) Who's that?

DIRECTOR: Balke, first class worker, 400 percent. Our best horse.

SCHORN: He helped to put my head under the axe in '44, our best horse. Give me a shot.

DIRECTOR: (*Pours him a shot.*) It's only 80 proof.

6b

(*Mess hall. Lunch hour. At the HO booth a sign: "Closed because of delivery." The sign with the slogan has been removed. The tables are covered with tablecloths. At the backwall, a blackboard with the inscription "Plant News." The board is empty.*)

GESCHKE: (*Spooning his soup.*) I'd have thrown such muck into my former exploiter's face.

KOLBE: Geschke, the hero!

ANOTHER ONE: There's meat in it.

KARRAS: Meat, he said. He's lost his marbles. That's hunger for you.

LEGOFVEAL: We always had leg of veal for Christmas Eve, until '44. (*To Karras.*) Ever had a leg of veal? It melts on your tongue if you braise it in butter.

KARRAS: Who paid for the leg of veal?

LEGOFVEAL: (*Giggling.*) The government. I was a civil servant.

ANOTHER ONE: And who paid for the government?

ZEMKE: (*To Legofveal:*) You've been a Nazi?

LEGOFVEAL: I had six kids, colleagues.

KARRAS: That's what you get from eating meat. (*Enter Miss Matz. She pins the newspaper page with Balke's picture on the blackboard. Karras looks on. The blackboard hangs rather high.*) I think there was meat in the soup. (*Laughter. Miss Matz exits quickly.*)

STETTINER: There hangs the model worker.

ZEMKE: (*Aloud.*) There he's coming in person, his back pocket stuffed with our money. (*He rips the newspaper page with Balke's picture off the board.*)

STETTINER: (*Takes cover, then.*) Scab. Class traitor.

GESCHKE: What does the handyman get, Balke? (*Balke gets his lunch, sits down. Those sitting at his table get up, first Karras and Zemke. Kolbe and Krüger remain seated.*)

KRUGER: Balke, I have nothing against you, and Stettiner was a Stormtrooper and he's an asshole. But that is true: you've stabbed us in the back.

BALKE: I didn't keep anything for myself.

STETTINER: That isn't fair, that's stupid.

BALKE: Everybody could do what I did.

KARRAS: Could.

BALKE: Yesterday at the meeting you couldn't stop carping: There are no shoes. If the workers at the shoe factories would make more shoes, we'd have more shoes.

A WORKER: Make a child if you're castrated.

SCHUREK: It depends on us if we achieve a better life.

KARRAS: I can read that in the paper my ass has a subscription for.

BALKE: You belong in the office with your smart ass. (*Laughter.*)

KRUGER: Depends on us, you say. Alright, we'll do our job. But who's skimming off? Did you see that union preacher at the meeting yesterday?

KOLBE: If you don't like him, why do you put up with him?

GESCHKE: Why do you think?

KOLBE: There is a worker sitting at the director's desk. You are a worker, too, and can talk to him.

KARRAS: And who accused Lerka of sabotage, for the accident? The worker at the director's desk. He got rid of the worker with his blue-collar shirt.

BALKE: That was no accident. You know that as well as I do. (*Pause.*) If you don't want to hear of the new norm, who then is cutting wages, you or me?

KOLBE: You only harm yourselves. We live as well as we work.

KRUGER: We're giving them a finger and they'll tear off our arm.

ZEMKE: (*To Balke.*) If you go on cutting wages, we'll beat you to a pulp.

7

(Street. Evening.)

SCHORN: We worked together at the munitions factory, Balke. They arrested me in '44: sabotage. They didn't arrest you. You were the informer.

BALKE: What makes you say informer? I was in testing. They had put me there, a supervisor right and left, so they could nail me. The hand grenades from your shop had faulty pins. I let them pass or marked them rejects, depending on where the snitches were. But it didn't stop. I was also for shortening the war, but they'd have shortened my head if it was discovered without my assistance.

SCHORN: *(Coldly.)* Maybe. *(Pause.)* What was the fight about in the mess hall at lunch time?

BALKE: That was against me. Scab, class traitor, and so forth.

(Pause.)

SCHORN: Tell me if they'll make it difficult for you.

(Pause.)

BALKE: What's past, can you forget it?
SCHORN: No.

8a

(Engineering office. Engineers Kant and Trakehner, the Director, Schorn, Balke, Bittner.)

DIRECTOR: Furnace Four has cracked. I don't need to explain what that means. The bombed furnaces aren't rebuilt yet. Materials are hard to come by. If one furnace isn't operative, our plan isn't worth its paper.

TRAKEHNER: It isn't worth it with or without Furnace Four.

DIRECTOR: That's a debatable point. You've checked the furnace. One thing is clear: it needs to be totally rebuilt, patching up won't do. That means: it won't be operative, four months at least, that's what it takes to rebuild. *(There is a knock at the door.)*

MISS MATZ: Excuse me. The journalist is here. He wants to see you.

He says he needs something about production for the Sunday magazine.

DIRECTOR: Tell him he should write about June bugs. That'll fascinate his readers in December. I have no use for him. Not now.

MISS MATZ: (*Giggles, then.*) But . . . (*The Director looks at her.*) Yes. June bugs. (*Exit.*)

DIRECTOR: It's customary to shut down the furnace for the time it's being rebuilt. That's the way it's always been done. (*Pause. Wipes his sweating forehead.*)

TRAKEHNER: I see no other way.

BITTNER: Right, that's the way it's always been done. (*Kant is silent.*)

DIRECTOR: If we're shutting down the furnace, we'll be in a hell of trouble. First of all, there are our delivery deadlines.

TRAKEHNER: Has it ever happened that they've been kept?

DIRECTOR: It has happened. Anyway, our production plan depends on Furnace Four. Shutting it down is impossible.

TRAKEHNER: Alright, but not shutting it down is also impossible.

DIRECTOR: That was my question.

KANT: You want to rebuild the furnace while it's burning?

DIRECTOR: Yes. The chamber they're working on will be shut down, of course.

TRAKEHNER: Nonsense.

BITTNER: If that is possible, the bosses would have done it.

TRAKEHNER: The Million Mark Question: who will collapse first, bricklayer or furnace.

KANT: It might be possible to work at 100 degrees Celsius. Question is: can you do quality work. I doubt it.

SCHORN: This isn't only a question of technology, of materials.

TRAKEHNER: "But a question of class consciousness." I won't presume to lecture you in these matters, you're the paid expert, after all. But we're dealing here with hard facts.

SCHORN: The working class is creating new facts.

TRAKEHNER: I take off my hat to the working class. But exploitation is not a new fact.

DIRECTOR: Bricklayer Balke offered to rebuild the furnace while it's burning. I think his proposal merits serious consideration.

TRAKEHNER: Balke is a crackpot.

SCHORN: Balke is a bricklayer.

TRAKEHNER: I understand. If a bricklayer rebuilds the furnace, he'll be a hero. If the furnace cracks, we'll be the saboteurs.

(*Schorn smiles.*)

BITTNER: The furnace is going to crack.

BALKE: It has cracked.

BITTNER: You think you won't crack, right?

TRAKEHNER: I won't accept the responsibility.

BALKE: I demand permission to rebuild the furnace.

(*Pause. Trakehner lights a cigar.*)

DIRECTOR: We'll get into a hell of trouble.

TRAKEHNER: You may think whatever you like of me. I've always done my duty.

DIRECTOR: More than that.

TRAKEHNER: Yes, even more. But that I should risk my reputation as an expert, that's going too far. Nobody can ask that of me. (*Pause.*) It's an idea for the wastebasket, a utopia.

BALKE: (*To the Director.*) I can rebuild the furnace without an engineer.

TRAKEHNER: As you please. (*He gets up.*) I'll find a job everywhere. It's no fun to build your Socialism. (*He extinguishes his cigar.*) Even the cigars are no fun.

SCHORN: You're right.

TRAKEHNER: What?

SCHORN: I said, you're right. But Balke can't do Furnace Four without an engineer. (*Pause. Trakehner sits down and re-lights his cigar.*)

KANT: (*To Balke.*) Did you do the calculations?

BALKE: (*Hands him papers.*) I've tried.

(*Pause. Kant is reading.*)

8b

(*Hall at the factory. Workers. The Director, Balke and Schurek facing them.*)

DIRECTOR: We have something truly great in mind. It will set an example of production for the whole country. We're going to prove with it what the working class is able to achieve. It ought to be an honor for you to participate. (*Pause.*)

SCHUREK: It's a job like any other job. It's only that it will be the first time.

A WORKER: Booze is booze, said the bartender and poured the turpentine.

KRUGER: That's exploitation.

BALKE: The plan depends on it, colleagues.

VOICE: (*From the background.*) We're shitting on the plan.

BALKE: Question is, if you have something to shit without the plan. (*Bespectacled Man laughs bleatingly, stifles it as nobody else laughs.*) I can't rebuild the furnace alone, but we need it. (*Silence.*)

DIRECTOR: Krüger, you said; exploitation. All your life you've been exploited. Today your boy is at the university.

KRUGER: Did I send him to the university? I was against it. (*Silence.*)

BALKE: It will be hard, very hot. Double pay, three times the work.

A WORKER: And eight years if something goes wrong, like with Lerka.

BITTNER: I'm telling you, they'll botch it.

BALKE: I know what I'm doing.

(*Pause.*)

KOLBE: I was sitting in a tank until '45. That was no icebox either. I'll join you.

KRUGER: (*Steps forward.*) If it's got to be . . .

8c

(*Factory yard. Stettiner, Geschke, then the Bespectacled Man, later Kolbe.*)

STETTINER: Do you need dry bricks, Geschke? There are lots at Furnace Four.

GESCHKE: Them Balke needs himself.

STETTINER: Exactly. (*Bespectacled Man comes from the mess hall, stops.*) Man, our wages will be screwed till 1980 if they finish that furnace. (*Kolbe comes from the mess hall with Balke's lunch. Stettiner says aloud.*) He even carries lunch into the furnace for his excellency, the foreman. That guy knows how to take care of himself.

KOLBE: If I find out who's pinched Balke's jacket so he can't get to the mess hall, from the hot furnace across the yard, I know what I'll do.

STETTINER: Mankind is evil.

(*Kolbe exits.*)

GESCHKE: Do you have the jacket?

STETTINER: If you need one, I'll make you a good price, Geschke. (*Geschke exits.*)

BESPECTACLED MAN: Good quality?

STETTINER: Hundred percent wool. Almost new.

8d

(*At the furnace. Balke and Krüger. They are exhausted. Kolbe arrives with Balke's lunch and beer.*)

KOLBE: (*Drinks.*) The tank was an icebox compared to the furnace.

BALKE: (*Eating.*) The furnace isn't a Nazi tank. You can get out.

KRUGER: (*To Kolbe.*) You've got the paper?

KOLBE: (*Pulls a paper from his pocket.*) Here. "Breakthrough at VEB RED OCTOBER. The workers of VEB RED OCTOBER achieved a breakthrough. Model worker Balke developed a plan to rebuild a circular furnace without interrupting production; this was regarded as impossible in the industry. Advocated by the chairman of the plant's union committee Schurek . . ."

KRUGER: Schurek, of all people.

KOLBE: ". . . the plan received enthusiastic support. It will save 400,000 Marks and guarantee that the plant's production goals are accomplished. We paid a visit to the brigade of the daring innovator at their workplace where we discovered lively activity and could steal a glance into the furnace. How these men handle their bricks, that's what I call a Socialist tempo . . ." Blockhead! You'll burn your paws without tempo. (*He reads on.*) "They're working with gloves since the bricks are white-hot, and care for the working man is always the focus. While one chamber after another is shut down, dismantled, and newly constructed, behind a thin wall the fire goes on burning next door. It has happened that the wooden clogs of the workers began to smolder. This is an achievement the layman can't imagine. Sweat is pouring down the naked torsos, faces express determination and confidence. The plant's employees are justly proud of these men.''

BALKE: That's why they steal the dry bricks we need.

KOLBE: If that scribbler should ever come again, we'll teach him a lesson. At 100 degrees Celsius in the furnace.

KRUGER: He made you look pretty important, Balke.

9

(*Furnace. Balke, Krüger, and Kolbe at work. Bespectacled Man walks by and throws a brick which hits Balke.*)

KRUGER: That's too much.

KOLBE: (*Picks up the brick.*) We'll save it. That's evidence.

BALKE: (*Rubbing the hit spot.*) Is it dry?

KOLBE: Yes.

BALKE: (*Grinning.*) The evidence will go into the wall. (*Kolbe hands him the brick.*)

10

(*Tavern. Street. Evening. The innkeeper is washing glasses. At the ruined wall a primitive drawing of a female nude. A young woman is standing next to it.*)

YOUNG MAN: (*Ambling by, passes the girl and walks back.*) Did you sit for this, Miss?

(*The young woman walks away quickly. The yelling of children playing war, coming closer. The young man jabs with one finger at the breasts of the drawing and follows the girl, whistling. Two boys with rusty helmets and gas masks, armed with the remains of a submachine gun. A third one, the smallest, drums on an empty pot.*)

FIRST BOY: (''*Shoots,*'' *yells.*) Dead!

SECOND BOY: Doesn't count.

FIRST: (*Attacks him and throws him on the ground.*) Give up your weapons. Now! (*They struggle for the weapons.*)

SECOND: I'm the Ami, and the Ami wins, my father says. (*He ''shoots.''*)

FIRST: Spoilsport!

SECOND: Coward. (*They exit, hitting each other. The third one follows, drumming. Two Gentlemen enter with briefcases.*)

FIRST GENTLEMAN: (*Walking.*) The way I see the situation, there'll definitely be a war. America won't allow this. Do you know what I've heard? (*He looks in all directions, starts to whisper.*)

SECOND GENTLEMAN: I'm told he said: war isn't inevitable. (*With raised forefinger.*) Not inevitable! (*The two gentlemen exit laughing. Two Construction Workers enter the tavern. The Innkeeper brings them beer.*)

FIRST CONSTRUCTION WORKER: One more week. Then we'll drink water.

SECOND: My fridge broke down, unemployed. Eight more installments.

INNKEEPER: The gentlemen are from the other side?

FIRST: Something wrong with that?

INNKEEPER: (*Lifts a glass with water.*) See what I'm drinking? Water. You think the innkeeper can afford to drink beer? Not here. Not in the East. Here, they're starving the middle class.

SECOND: (*Tips his finger at the Innkeeper's belly.*) Is that water, too?

INNKEEPER: It's no laughing matter for the small businessman. Better unemployed but free.

FIRST: Agreed. We'll take the tavern. (*To the second.*) Tell him to show you the books, Hanke! (*To the Innkeeper.*) You've got a mortgage?

INNKEEPER: Be glad you're not in my position.

CONSTRUCTION WORKER: Retracting? That'll cost damages.

INNKEEPER: (*Laughs sheepishly.*) 'Cause it's you. One round.

(*The Construction Workers finish their beer and leave. Karras and Zemke enter the tavern. The Innkeeper brings beer and shots.*)

ZEMKE: You've got a cigarette left? Thanks.

KARRAS: Balke hasn't given in yet, that mad dog.

ZEMKE: He needs to be reminded. (*Karras is silent.*) Tonight he's working late again. He goes home on his bicycle, alone. He's got to pass here.

KARRAS: Balke is a tough customer.

ZEMKE: He's scum. I know. I was red like no one else. With fist and chair legs for the World Revolution. They've hit me over the head and kicked my ass, the police and the army. I said: Alright, it's for the World Revolution. Then I noticed, our leaders didn't stick their necks out. When I noticed that . . .

KARRAS: You joined the Stormtroopers.

ZEMKE: How's that?

KARRAS: You're trying to tell me you weren't a Stormtrooper?

ZEMKE: None of your business. (*Pause.*) Party is party. It's all the same. Empty promises and stuffing their safes with the worker's cash. We've got to do the World Revolution ourselves, Karras. No rain is going to wash that off.

KARRAS: Balke screwed up our norm. He's getting eight Marks an hour for it, and a reminder from me that he won't fit into his furnace again. But you can do your World Revolution alone, Zemke.

ZEMKE: Scared?

KARRAS: Not me.

ZEMKE: I'd make twenty Marks an hour if I wanted to. But I won't let them bullshit me. (*Pause.*)

KARRAS: We've warned him. (*He walks to the door, looks down the street.*) He's coming. (*They step out and walk towards Balke.*) Get off, Balke.

BALKE: (*Brakes his bicycle and gets off.*) What do you want? You're drunk.

KARRAS: We've warned you, Balke.

BALKE: What do you want? (*Zemke hits him. The bicycle falls to the ground. His back to the ruined wall.*) You're hitting yourselves, right into your own face.

(*Zemke and Karras keep hitting him.*)

11

(*Office. Schorn, Director.*)

SCHORN: If Balke's dropping out, who'll take charge of the furnace?

DIRECTOR: (*Hesitant.*) It's the first time that a furnace is rebuilt while on fire.

SCHORN: That means: it won't be done without Balke?

DIRECTOR: Not yet.

SCHORN: Much depends on him. Too much. (*Pause.*) I've worked with him in the munitions industry, hand grenades. His hand grenades were always right. He was a good worker. He didn't sabotage German rearmament. I'm asking myself: will he sabotage reconstruction?

(*Enter Stettiner.*)

DIRECTOR: What do you want?
STETTINER: I'd like to ask if my improvement proposal has already been checked. It's not the bonus I'm asking for.
DIRECTOR: For what then?
STETTINER: We have a workers' government, don't we? I'm a worker.
DIRECTOR: We don't work for the government. You'll get a notice when your proposal has been checked.
STETTINER: (*Doesn't leave.*) I was a Stormtrooper, that's right. Hitler did bullshit me. Now we have a workers' government.
DIRECTOR: (*Bluntly.*) What do you want?
STETTINER: I'd like to join. The party.

(*The Director is silent. Pause.*)

SCHORN: Here, there's a form. Fill it in. (*Stettiner exits with the form.*)
DIRECTOR: Twice workers' government (*looks at his watch*) in three minutes. That's too much.
SCHORN: Three new members in one year. That's too few.
DIRECTOR: Fewer might be more.

12

(*At the furnace. Balke, marks of the beating on his face, Kolbe, and a Doctor are standing in front of Krüger who is very pale and sits on a stack of bricks, his back leaning against another stack. At some distance, Bittner, Karras, Zemke, and others. Krüger is breathing hard.*)

DOCTOR: I've told you this way of working is suicide. But you won't listen to the doctor until you're in a coffin. (*To Krüger.*) Listen, man, leave the furnace alone. You, Balke, also belong in a hospital bed rather than in that furnace.

BALKE: I believe you don't know what's at stake, doctor.

DOCTOR: The better future built on the workers' bones, right?

KRUGER: (*With effort.*) You should have told that to the Nazis, doctor.

DOCTOR: I'm ordering you to keep silent, Krüger, you'll get a hemmorhage.

KRUGER: Just now you said I already have one.

DOCTOR: Another word and you'll have it. What happened to your skull, Balke? Did you try to push your head through the wall again? The wall was stronger, what?

BALKE: The wall was me.

(*Karras exits. Two workers enter with a stretcher. They carry Krüger off, followed by the Doctor and Kolbe. The onlookers disperse. Bittner and a Young Worker remain. Balke sits down on the bricks.*)

YOUNG WORKER: Bittner, what do you think, are they going to make it? (*Bittner shrugs his shoulders.*) Shall we bet. I say: they'll make it.

BITTNER: I never bet. (*The Young Worker exits. Bittner steps to Balke, offers him a cigarette. Balke takes a fresh pack from his pocket.*) Do you have a replacement for Krüger, Balke? (*Balke is silent.*) I would join you. What's got to be, got to be. (*Balke is silent.*) It's like that: I thought I've laid bricks for furnaces for thirty years, I know everything about furnaces, and no one is fooling me.

BALKE: And if you're wrong again?

BITTNER: You want to do the furnace alone, Balke?

BALKE: (*Gets up.*) Did I say that? I don't mind if you join us.

BITTNER: Shall we go together? (*They exit. Stettiner and the Bespectacled Man walk by.*)

STETTINER: If someone gets the idea to throw enough bricks into the gas duct, I'd really feel sorry for Balke and the furnace.

13

(*At the furnace. Balke, Schorn.*)

BALKE: Bricks in the gas duct. That spells: three days' delay. Our plan is shot. (*Pause.*) I'm asking myself, how long will the furnace

remain standing. I'm going to give up before they blow it up.
They laughed about the dumb model worker. They've thrown
bricks at me. They've beaten me up in the street. I won't be their
patsy.

SCHORN: Whose? (*Silence.*) Do you know who's thrown those
bricks into the gas duct? (*Silence.*)

BALKE: What's going to happen if I say the name?

SCHORN: You've got to know what you want, Balke.

BALKE: I'm no informer.

SCHORN: You've got to know what you want. The factories are ours,
and the state and its power. We'll lose it if we don't use it.
(*Silence.*)

BALKE: It was Spectacles.

14

(*Mess hall. Workers, the Saleswoman.*)

ZEMKE: First Lerka, now Spectacles. That's too much.

STETTINER: That's workers' power. (*Exits.*)

GESCHKE: Yes, we won't stand for it.

ANOTHER ONE: What can we do?

A YOUNG WORKER: We'll strike.

AN OLDER ONE: We'd cut into our own flesh.

ZEMKE: I know one who sits in the minister's office. Under Hitler he
was like that—(*He shows a match.*) Now his size is extra large and
every week he needs a new suit. That's the flesh we cut into. He
who works is a traitor. (*Siren. The Older Worker exits.*)

AN OLD ONE: I'll bet he's getting the police on our heads.

(*Some workers exit.*)

A WORKER: (*To the Old One.*) You wouldn't care. Your eldest one
is with the police, isn't he?

OLD ONE: Yes, he's already a lieutenant. (*He gets up and slowly
walks out. Two others follow him.*)

ZEMKE: He who works is a traitor. (*Pause. He steps to the HO
booth.*) Beer. (*The Saleswoman leaves the booth and locks it up.*)
What's that supposed to mean?

SALESWOMAN: (*Dryly.*) Strike. (*Exits.*)

A WORKER: That's too much.

(*Another one gets up and leaves. Enter Balke.*)

ZEMKE: There, the informer's coming.
BALKE: (*To Bittner and Kolbe.*) Won't you start working?
ZEMKE: (*Plants himself in front of Balke.*) We don't work with an informer.

(*Bittner and Kolbe are silent. Balke exits. Zemke spits on the floor. Pause.*)

A WORKER: I just don't want to kill myself, that's all. Piecework is murder.

(*Zemke has broken into the HO booth, he drags a case of beer out. While doing it, he steps on packaged butter.*)

KARRAS: Step off the butter, Zemke.
ZEMKE: I shit on butter. (*The workers, except for Karras, Bittner, and Legofveal, get themselves beer.*) What's wrong with you, Legofveal.
LEGOFVEAL: I've got no cash.
ZEMKE: This is for free, stupid. People's Own Plant Zemke.

(*Legofveal gets himself a beer. Enter Balke, Schorn, the Director, with a few workers.*)

SCHORN: Take the beer back. (*Zemke drinks with big gulps, looking at Schorn. The workers, one after the other, drink with some hesitation. Kolbe, a bottle in his hand, doesn't drink.*) What do you want?
ZEMKE: (*Drinks a second bottle.*) Justice.
OTHERS: Where is Spectacles?
　　　　Where is Lerka?
　　　　The norm has to go.
　　　　Piecework is murder.
SCHORN: (*Points at the trampled butter.*) The butter has to go, too?

(*Pause.*)

A WORKER: What's the butter got to do with the norm?
SCHORN: No norm, no butter.
A WORKER: No butter, no norm.
SCHORN: Who's setting prices?

ZEMKE: Your talk won't make us drunk.

SCHORN: You'll take care of that yourselves, right?

DIRECTOR: Go to your work.

ZEMKE: Not without Spectacles.

DIRECTOR: The sabotage cost us twenty thousand.

SCHORN: That's our money. And you're shouting ''Freedom'' for the guy who took it from us.

ZEMKE: Sweet talk, they always were good at that when their own jobs were at stake. He who works is a traitor.

BALKE: And what's at stake for you, loudmouth?

SCHORN: You can go, Zemke.

(*Pause.*)

ZEMKE: I'll do as I please. (*He puts the beer bottle in his pocket and walks towards the door.*)

SCHORN: The beer has to be paid for.

(*Zemke comes back, throws the money on the ledge of the booth, exits. Silence.*)

DIRECTOR: Go to your work.

(*Some workers put money on the ledge at the booth and leave.*)

GESCHKE: (*To Schorn.*) You've crammed yourself with politics, secretary. They have no Socialism in America, only workers who drive their own car. Socialism, that's shoes on ration cards. Explain that to me.

SCHORN: The worker owns the car. But who owns the workers? We're getting our shoes on ration cards. But we own the car factories.

AN OLD WORKER: You know how to talk. But who says it's true?

(*Enter Schurek, he hangs a banner which reads: ''The working class demands the raising of norms.''*)

SCHORN: If you don't understand it, we'll all go to hell.

KARRAS: Geschke is asking for shoes. (*He lifts Geschke's foot to show the torn shoe.*) Here. It's 10 degrees below outside. You want to silence him with car factories. We're protesting that you raise the norm without ever asking us. You're hanging a banner in front of our nose: ''The working class demands the raising of norms.'' Socialism is left by the wayside.

SCHORN: We're protecting your interest when we're raising norms.

KARRAS: A bricklayer blows up a furnace. You say: saboteur. Good riddance. Did you explain to him why the model worker is getting 400 percent and he only pocket money? Why is Schurek getting fat since he is protecting our interest?

SCHORN: Who elected Schurek?

A WORKER: Not forever.

(Schurek disappears.)

SCHORN: *(Grins.)* Elect a commission to investigate why Schurek is getting fat since he's protecting your interest.

DIRECTOR: Don't forget to pay for the beer.

GESCHKE: And what about the norm?

SCHORN: *(Pointing at the banner.)* If you want the bosses back, tear that down. *(Workers put money on the ledge of the booth.)* Where's the saleswoman?

A WORKER: She heard we're striking.

ANOTHER ONE: Closed the shop and disappeared.

LEGOFVEAL: No discipline. That calls for a severe reprimand.

GESCHKE: *(To Legofveal.)* Who's paying for the butter you've pinched, Councilor?

LEGOFVEAL: *(Empties his pockets.)* I was only Inspector.

(Workers exit. Bittner, Kolbe, Karras remain behind. Karras takes a bottle of beer, pays, sits down and drinks.)

DIRECTOR: *(To Balke, Bittner, and Kolbe.)* How long do you need to repair the damage?

BALKE: Three days.

DIRECTOR: And our deadline?

BALKE: We can do it if we work fast. *(Bittner nods.)*

KOLBE: I won't have anything to do with that saboteur, but I won't work with an informer.

(Pause.)

BALKE: Then it will take five days, and we won't make the deadline.

KOLBE: Working in Furnace Four is volunteer work. *(He stops at the door.)*

DIRECTOR: Karras, what about you? You're a furnace bricklayer.

KARRAS: (*Looking at Balke who turns away.*) Balke cooked this mess up, let him eat it now.

SCHORN: Balke didn't go into the furnace for his own fun.

(*Pause.*)

KARRAS: When do you want me to start?

(*Kolbe exits.*)

BALKE: You couldn't stop carping about the scab who's cutting your wages, you refused to understand what's at stake here. You've thrown bricks at me. I've put them into the furnace wall. You've beaten me up, you and Zemke, when I came from the furnace. And if I have to lay bricks with my teeth, with you never. (*Silence.*)

KARRAS: Maybe he did go into the furnace for his own fun. (*He exits. Silence.*)

SCHORN: You won't lay bricks with your teeth, Balke.

BALKE: I can't work with Karras.

SCHORN: Who asked me if I can work with you?

15

(*Factory gate. Morning. Karras enters, followed by Balke.*)

BALKE: I need you, Karras. I don't ask as a friend. You've got to help me.

KARRAS: (*Stops.*) I thought you wanted to build Socialism all by yourself. When do we start?

BALKE: Why not right away. We don't have much time.

(*They walk through the factory gate. Kolbe enters and follows them.*)

1956   Collaborator: Inge Müller

TRACTOR

TRACTOR (*Traktor*) was written in the years 1955 to 1961. In 1974, on the occasion of its first printing, the author wrote or selected from various sources the poems and prose pieces inserted between the scenes, creating a montage which juxtaposes the original work with comments on its content and the process of its writing. The definitive text was published in *Geschichten aus der Produktion 2, Rotbuch 126,* Berlin, 1974. The play was first produced at the Friedrich Wolf Theater, Neustrelitz, April 27, 1975, in Thomas Vallentin's staging. Its West German premiere soon followed at the Ulm Theatre, September 27, 1975, directed by Walter Pfaff.

In retrospect, the text of TRACTOR in its published form marks two turning points in Müller's development: the step from a more or less realistic dialogue and dramaturgy, as in THE SCAB and THE CORRECTION, both of which were written in the 1950s, to an adoption of classic models using verse, or otherwise heightened language, and a corresponding structure. During the sixties, the playwright explored and developed the classic mode further in such works as THE CONSTRUCTION SITE, PHILOCTETES, PRO-METHEUS, and THE HORATIAN. Then, in 1974, the published text of TRACTOR presented the first example of a dramaturgic model Müller called "synthetic fragment," a form he further experimented with in such plays as GERMANIA DEATH IN BERLIN and THE TASK, and which was most fully realized in his HAMLETMACHINE.

TRACTOR focuses on two themes: firstly, the hardships prevailing during the early postwar years in the Soviet-occupied zone of the former Reich, today's East Germany. Here under very difficult conditions the first tentative moves towards a socialist economy and society were made, with a people which in its majority had actively supported the Nazi regime. The second theme is the struggle between old modes of thinking and working, which resist change, and a new way of life. Both themes converge in the story of the play's "hero" who—refusing to be a hero—is literally "torn" by the conflict between his personal ''pursuit of happiness'' and the socialist concept of a communal good. The mines buried in fallow fields and the dog-eat-dog mentality entrenched in frightened minds were both inherited from fascist rule and its war, and their necessary removal was in each case as difficult, as it often was dangerous.

The contradiction between the individual's desires and the claims made by historical progress, both as inevitable as they are justified, is a recurrent topic in Müller's work, even if his perspective of it has changed greatly over the years. In TRACTOR, the progressive socialist resolution of the contradiction clearly is envisioned, and not only as an utopia. However, the price that is to be paid for such progress is equally brought into view.

Several aspects of the text need clarification for readers who aren't familiar with the history of East Germany from 1945 to 1948:

A ''tractorist'' is, of course, the operator of a tractor; the term reminds us of ''motorist.'' The word was borrowed from the Russian and often signified a tractor operator working for a M.A.S. (Maschinen-Ausleih-Station, meaning ''Lending Station for Machinery'')—pools of tractors and other farming machinery which were owned and operated by a government agency. There, farmers could apply for tractors and other machines, including the needed driver or mechanic, to have them work their fields.

The ''secret weapons'' referred to by the Sergeant Major were the miracle weapons Hitler kept promising during the last months of the war, weapons which supposedly would stop the Russian advance and defeat the Allied forces.

''. . . old fields allotted to another kind of people.'' A reference to the land reform (Bodenreform) which was implemented in the Soviet-occupied Zone during the fall of 1945. All large estates with an acreage of more then 250 acres were expropriated. Two-thirds of the land was distributed among farm hands, small farmers, or refugees from the eastern parts of the former Reich—since 1945 belonging to Czechoslovakia, Poland, or Russia—while one-third was used to establish state-run farming enterprises.

''Activist'' is the term for a model worker in a state-run plant or a collective enterprise, as the probably more familiar Russian term ''Stakhanovite'' was.

''Brandenburg'' was a largely agricultural province that encompassed Berlin; in 1952 it was divided into several administrative districts.

The reference to the ''grandchildren'' one has to stoop to reflects the then widely accepted concept of a German collective guilt for the crimes committed by the Nazi system.

''Brigade'' is the term for teams of workers—in this case tractorists—who work together in a coordinated fashion; brigades usually stayed together for extended periods of time.

''You amputated of all nations'' is a derisive misquoting of the Communist slogan ''Proletarians of all nations, unite.''

''Lending station for bone parts'': a mocking reference to the lending stations for farm machinery.

The first two scenes were written in a doggerel as it first appeared in early German farces written during the Renaissance by Hans Sachs and others. It serves to emphasize the prologue function of the two brief scenes.

Note on the sources of inserted quotes:

Helden der Arbeit (Heroes of Labor) was a book on model workers, the term ''Held der Arbeit'' is an honorary title for exemplary workers.

Dziga Vertov: famous Russian who was one of the earliest documentary filmmakers.

Ernst Thälmann: the leader of the German Communist Party (KPD) in the twenties and thirties, he was murdered by the Nazis in 1945 at Buchenwald Concentration Camp.

C. W.

SOME WERE HANGING FROM THE LAMPPOSTS, TONGUE PROTRUDING
IN FRONT OF THEIR BELLY THE SIGN   I'M A COWARD

(*Field. Snow.*)

SERGEANT MAJOR:
    And so I tell you since you may not know it:
    It's just a ruse of war if we retreat.
    Because it won't take longer than a fortnight
    Till secret weapons wipe out Russia.
    And so the enemy sees we won't give up
    We must lay mines, that'll make him stop.
    Dig faster so I won't freeze over.
    (*Soldiers dig.*)
                   Hey

    Why don't you dig?
SOLDIER: (*Who doesn't dig.*)
                   Because I see
    What grows here are potatoes, seems to me.
    (*Soldiers stop digging.*)
    And so I think they might be needed when
    There's peace and chimneys are to smoke again.

SERGEANT MAJOR:
>I've heard you. Watch now what will happen here.
>You there. This is high treason, plain and clear.
>What are you gaping at. Go get
>A rope and break the traitor's neck.

>*The emperor needs soldiers, father.*
>*Stop up your ears, son*
>*So you cannot hear the drum*
>*And cover yourself with manure to the crown of your head*
>*So you won't be blinded by the arms' glitter.*[1]

It was the First of May when the activist got his medal, a month later the explosion blew him up. His leg had to be amputated . . . "But I still do those five acres. You can't take that away from me. I think a lot of people could line up and receive potato rations if we still finish those five acres."[2]

ANOTHER KIND OF CONVERSATION WAS HELD ON THE OLD FIELDS ALLOTTED TO ANOTHER KIND OF PEOPLE

1

FARMER:
>That was the war. Today a year has passed
>People are starving and the field lies waste.
>But no one dares to take to it the plow.

TRACTORIST: I say there are still mines below
FARMER: I say the people in the cities starve.
TRACTORIST: Are shattered bones something for them to carve.
FARMER: I think all mines have been removed by now.
TRACTORIST: Then try! You plow!
FARMER:
>   If I only knew how
>To drive a tractor!

TRACTORIST:
>   Don't you have a horse?
>Look at the hero! Now he's quiet, of course.

FARMER:
>This field here would be best for spuds.

And that for wheat. What lacks is guts.
TRACTORIST:
    Listen. During the war I've risked a lot
    And didn't ask for whom or on what spot.
    There's peace now and I ask: Is this field mine?
FARMER:I ask you, does the sky rain bread, a gift divine?

2

FARMER:
    I've got a stretch of wasteland, tractorist
    It wasn't plowed since '45. I need it.
TRACTORIST:
    I've got my bones here, farmer, forty sound ones
    Saved in four years of war, not one too many.
    I need them too. I never did like mines.
FARMER: Who's talking mines.
TRACTORIST:
          Whoever hits them won't.
    In Brandenburg it was my pal, for instance.
    We stood around the tractors in the evening
    The peace was one year old and we were twenty
    We smoked, some farmers were with us, complaining
    About a scrap of wasteland, full of mines.
    I said: I still need my bones for a while
    You need the field, go with your horses at it
    I don't like mines, you know. Said my pal:
    I don't like hunger pangs, throws down his butt
    Jumps on the tractor and away he drives.
    Drove straight to heaven, the tractor, too, was gone.
FARMER: (*Takes off his cap.*)
    I pity him. It always hits the wrong ones.
TRACTORIST: You want to dig him up? I'll show you where.
FARMER:
    He wasn't merely cracking jokes. He pulled
    His hands out of his pockets when a field
    Needed the plow.
TRACTORIST:
          That's true, and he himself
    Is now plowed into by the maggots down there

Won't crack a joke no more and won't need pockets.
FARMER:
    He'd do it once again if he stood here
    And even if they hadn't swept today.
TRACTORIST:
    I see! He now plants on my neck the corpse
    Who's eaten wreaths and now fattens the flowers.
    You do the same old song and dance? I love it:
    If nothing works, no horse, no tractor, and no
    Talking, they harness up the dear departed
    While otherwise they'd rather shit on them.
    A Dead horse pulls more than ten tractors could.
    Why should I be the one to risk my limbs
    I didn't lay the mines.
FARMER: I didn't either.
TRACTORIST:
    And if the hunger of all Brandenburg
    Is marching to your field, shouting for bread
    Those not yet born and all those putrefied
    Limping along and shouting without voice
    And if it's half the world that roars with hunger
    To me your field is of less worth than my corpse
    You plow your mine field with your own bones.
FARMER: (*Puts his cap on.*)
    What he has done, he would do once again.
TRACTORIST:Let me tell you: the dead have the last laugh.

INVITATION TO DANCE OR WRESTLING THE ANGEL

TRACTORIST:
    You won't ride me down into your pit. I'm
    No hero. Get off my neck, maggot fodder.
    Plowman of mines who's plowed now by his field.
    Where did you lose your flesh, old bones. If you
    Had listened to me, you'd still be in one piece.
    Get lost, I am not greedy for your wreaths.
    What do you want. Stopping my ticker with
    Your ruptured hide bag spilling out its bones
    Won't make you younger, only dogs shit backwards.

Is it my fault you can't drink beer no more.
I didn't talk you into your ascension.
How long are we supposed to stoop before
Our grandchildren, as each one of us
Carries a pile of corpses on his back
And each one's pregnant with his own carcass.
Ride others, hero, I won't be your nag.
Go lift your ass of hot air off my back
My own behind is weight enough for me.
Get off or I'll show you where your place is.
You're the majority but I'm above you
What mother earth holds on to, runs her course
There is no resurrection till she stops
The flesh is going to her school of maggots.
And now I'll show you what you are. You are
Dirt at my boot heel, field that will be plowed.

I was a hero, my fame enormous
The four winds were roaring in my banners
When my drums were beaten the people fell silent
I have squandered my life.[3]

It was a known fact that this terrain was heavily contaminated. Sixteen mines already had been recovered. You had the scary feeling that more were still buried there. The colleagues searched the terrain one more time. They found nothing but not one of us liked to start working. Paul said: "Alright, then I'll plow. It doesn't matter so much if it hits me. The young ones still have a life to live. We're already over the hill." He lowered his plow. Suddenly Hans L. stepped forward, the youngest member of the brigade. He has been driving a tractor since he was sixteen. In dangerous terrain, he always sat only halfway on his seat so he could jump off if need be. Hans L. didn't want to avoid the challenge and took the lead position. It was to be done quickly. The last five acres of wasteland couldn't take forever, after all. His engine clattered into action. Paul A. followed him with his 45-Lanz-Bulldog at a distance of approximately sixty feet. The first tractor had finished one run when suddenly a resounding detonation was heard. Paul's plow had cut into a mine. It exploded and tore his tractor apart. Paul A. flew, without letting go of the steering wheel, about sixty feet up into the air. He said that he had experienced a similar feeling as a child when he jumped down from a high hay stack. While coming down it felt as if he was dreaming. The same way he had felt here now. Only this time he fainted afterwards . . . He told it all as if it couldn't have been any other way . . .[4]

PLOWING MINES

TRACTORIST:
>   The world a waste. The only plowman I.
>   Eternal tractorist, how long is eternal.
>   Weeds grow above and mines grow underneath
>   And faster than my furrow grow the weeds
>   Unto my back, unto my shoulders and
>   Into my eyes, into my teeth
>   And mine following mine ripped by my plowshare
>   Explodes and blows to heaven: me.
>   The field is made of glass, the dead are staring
>   Up at me from their hollowed empty eyeholes
>   And clearly through the dead of the last war
>   There shine the dead from all the other wars
>   In endless lines they're slowly drifting by
>   Washed by the subsoil water. But why me,
>   Under my plow the wasteland has no limit
>   And there's no limit to the endless line
>   Of hollow stomachs opened wide for feeding.
>   My dead pal, he is growing from my back now
>   The mine plower who's been plowed by the wasteland
>   He's ridden by the men who laid the mines
>   And one grows from another, carcass on
>   Top of carcass, the dead proliferate
>   And pile up straight into the heavens.
>   The tractor I sit on is shrinking
>   And I am shrinking underneath my load
>   The weeds like pincers grab the tractor
>   Green jaws are chewing steel to scrap iron
>   The dead are laughing from their rotten bellies
>   Each has a tier of corpses in his baggage

And then the field takes me under its plow and
We're one, a lump of carrion and scrap metal
That spins in nowhere and in emptiness.

*The feeling of failure, the awareness of defeat is thorough when you
read the old texts again. The temptation to blame the subject matter
for the failure, the material (a cannibal vocabulary—''We are such
stuff as dreams are made of''), the story of the amputated hero: it
could happen to anyone, it doesn't mean a thing; with one person
blood poisoning is sufficient, the next one has greater luck: he
needs a war. The excuse: Europe is a ruin, the dead aren't counted
amidst the ruins. The truth is concrete, I'm breathing stones. People
who do their work so that they can buy their bread don't have the
time for such musings. But hunger doesn't concern me. The im-
possibility of catching the event through its description; the incom-
patibility of writing and reading; the exorcism of the reader from the
text. Puppets stuffed with words instead of sawdust. Heartflesh. The
desire for a language no one can read is growing. Who is no one. A
language without words. Or the disappearance of the world in the
words. Instead: the lifelong compulsion to see, the bombardment of
images (Tree House Woman), the eyelids blasted off. Confronted
with the gnashing of teeth, the burning and singing. The slag heap
of literature in your back.*

The extinction of the world in the images.

THE SCREAM

TRACTORIST:
    Where am I. Black is all that I'm seeing.
    Did I say see. How do you know, my friend
    If you still have the eyes for black or white.
    Is it night or am I down below me
    Where there's no difference between day and night
    And between me and me no difference either.
    This is a bed. It's made of iron. Were it
    I, I wouldn't lie on it. And this is
    Me. Or what's left of me after the mine
    Age thirty-one, a tractorist from Gatow

Who was promoted yesterday to be a
Plowman of mines because he volunteered,
Eater of wreaths tomorrow. Offal. I
Was five foot six. And how tall am I now.
Am I talking with my mouth or without one.
Why does my voice sound as of yesterday.
He screams. As if a whole depot of mines
Blast after blast is blowing up inside him.
Hey, pal, do you hear how the angels sing.
Give up. You won't drown their voice with your screaming.
Be glad you can still scream. I can't no more.
He doesn't stop. Screams like a thousand men.
His voice is booming in my skull. And now
I'll tell you something: What is screaming there
Isn't beside, above, behind, below you
And you won't see it with your eyes if you
Screw your head every way and off your neck
Without eyes you know which man's face it is
If what is screaming there still has a face left
And if it has no face you'll see that too
His name is written on your ID card
His voice comes out of you, you are what's screaming
In that ruin that was your blood and flesh
Before the mine had blown you from this world
And everything you are is my pain and
What's keeping me together is your scream.

Communism begins where simple workers, conquering their hard chores, worry in a selfless manner about increasing the productivity of their work, about protecting each pood of grain, coal, iron, and other products, which are of no gain to the worker himself or to people "close to him," but to people "far from him," that is: to all of society as a whole.[5]

The textile worker must see the machine worker when he builds the loom for him. The worker of the machine shop must see the collier when he mines the fuel for his plant. The collier must see the farmer who plants the grain that feeds him.

All members of the working class must see each other if they are to establish a close, indestructible bond among themselves . . .[6]

HOSPITAL

1

NURSE: Five minutes only.

VISITOR: How are you doing.

TRACTORIST: Did you run into my leg on your way. I'm missing one or I can't count to two anymore. You count.

VISITOR: I bring you greetings from all of us.

TRACTORIST: Ask them if anyone could spare a leg.

VISITOR: They all know what you've done for us.

TRACTORIST: Tell them I regret it and won't do it again.

VISITOR: K. finished your furrow. There wasn't much left. Tomorrow we start sowing. Wheat. In S. at the new school, the children are writing essays about you: The tractorist P. A., our role model. And in the paper they write you're a hero.

TRACTORIST: Rip off your leg and you get in the paper. P. A. the one-legged role model. I'm no hero. I want my leg back.

VISITOR: You'll get used to the prosthesis. They make good ones now. That's what they've learned in the war, how to make a good prosthesis. I've brought you cigarettes and the paper.

TRACTORIST: I'll wrap your paper around the stump.

VISITOR: Well, the worst is over now for you. Eight more days and you're back on your legs.

TRACTORIST: On one leg.

2

NURSE: Five minutes only.

TRACTORIST: What do you want. You've got a mine field left?

VISITOR 2:
We now get tractors from the Ukraine.
Brand new out of the ashes, we arsonists.

TRACTORIST:
And all the heavens will tomorrow be
A Plant Owned By The People, just because
I've plowed a mine field, right. Amen.
Now tell me where I can get a new leg.

VISITOR 2:

    Bygones are bygones, but today's tomorrow
    And if we must be talking of the heavens
    You may think you're just dirt compared to it
    I tell you then: The heavens is the sky
    A hole with crows in it, above them stars.
    You are the dirt all things revolve around
    Even the globe itself, slowly or fast
    And faster with each furrow we are plowing
    Into its crust left gray by our parents
    And slowed down by each fallow if it stays gray
    You are the tractor, pull it from its rut.

TRACTORIST:

    With one leg 'cause the other's in the paper.
    If I could turn back time, I'd take back each
    And every furrow, and your globe is not
    Too steep a price for my sound leg, to my mind.

VISITOR 2:

    My globe. You walk a different one? Your leg.
    Because the men who made the mines thought like that
    And those who planted them fearing the rope and
    Dreading the hunger of three kids at night
    That's why you lie here with one leg too few.
    They didn't ask who's blown to smithereens
    By their work, as long as they got paid.
    Their kitchen stove was fueled in advance
    With Warsaw Rotterdam Vitebsk and Dresden.
    They let whole nations go up through the chimney.
    And then they hung their wives up in the smoke
    Paid with their own blood for their daily beer
    And fed the kids with their grandchildren.
    But also those who swept the mines, they'd checked
    Weeds and topsoil with more careful eyes
    For mines and pulled the last one from the ground
    With tooth and nail, had it been their own field.
    The globe doesn't revolve around your stump
    Nor round my backbone bent by SS steel rods.
    Since Man is more than what his bones add up to.

NURSE: I said five minutes.

VISITOR 2:   We ain't finished yet.

NURSE: He is a patient, you. He needs his sleep.

VISITOR 2:

He's lost a leg and that's more than enough.
Shall I leave him here now without a head
Alone with your and his own ignorance.
For legs there is prosthetics. He who can't walk
Can ride a car, the engine walks for him
Science helps us out where nature fails.
Whoever has no arm can borrow one from
His fellow man. Nobody lives alone here
No man has hand and foot just for himself
If he has none for his fellow man.
I know what our patient needs, his head.
And mine.

NURSE: Why don't you leave your head right here.

VISITOR 2:

One head was quite enough for a thousand bodies
As long as of the thousand-one a thousand
Served as manure for one, the thousand-first.
Today Man is no Man with only one head.
And if he has a thousand arms, he bends
With thousand arms his neck only a thousand
Times deeper under his own foot, he stamps
With thousand legs himself into the ground
And feeds his way with each of his own steps.

TRACTORIST: (*Laughs.*)

Don't go away. You learn a lesson here.
The brave new man is what's invented here.
He's the machine-man. How about a test.
Have you ever done it with a tractor.
Sing on: You amputated of all nations.
Nurse, I'm a lending station for bone parts.

NURSE: I'll complain about you to the doctor.

VISITOR 2:

I know what she'll tell the doctor now.
There is a madman sitting in room nine and
What you think I know, too.

TRACTORIST:
>   I know it better.
>   If someone's mad here it is me.

(*Pause.*)

VISITOR 2:
>   I also would prefer if I were Jesus
>   Who made the cripples walk, the dead alive.
>   He washed the world clean with his blood, the Bible
>   Tells us, and he is blessed who believes it.
>   It didn't last, the old filth soon was rising
>   And our sweat salts better than his blood.

TRACTORIST:
>   I'm Jesus too. Devour, it's my flesh.
>   I see them crowding the communion table
>   All those who built and those who laid the mines
>   They were full in advance, I paid for it
>   And now they feast again and I'm still paying.
>   Also my colleagues who dug up the mines
>   Look how collectively they pick my shinbone.
>   I watch them eat now and I hear them laugh
>   Their belly laughs about the idiot
>   Who filled them though he wasn't himself hungry.

VISITOR 2:
>   You're not the only one who suffers losses.
>   And many had to eat many a stew
>   They didn't cook.

TRACTORIST: Who do you tell that.

VISITOR 2:
>   You.
>   We were in transport on the Rennsteig highway
>   From one camp to another concentration
>   Camp, in trucks, Storm Troopers our guards
>   Handcuffed we traveled through the fatherland.
>   It was springtime. All the German birds were
>   On active duty, and the German forest
>   Was green as only German trees are, only
>   The wind was without fatherland, and we.
>   Our guards were thirsty, had the transport stop

At every second pub, filled up with beer
Then took a leak and guzzled beer again.
For us, they had a wonderful idea.
At every stop they showed us to the people
So they could spit at us. You see the traitors.
They want to rob the German mother of
Her child, the German husband of his wife.
And so forth from their hymn book. And they came
Babies in bellies, babies on their arms
And spit their venom into our face.
We couldn't wipe it off, being handcuffed.
They made us kneel in front of every child.
I couldn't see, with all the German spittle
The German country's beauty any longer.
TRACTORIST: Why are you telling me that. Am I Hitler.
VISITOR 2:
When we crawled from the camps, we had been sifted
With gas and quarries, from the barbed wire
Our way home took us through leveled cities.
On our bones they had erected them
And now we had the ruins on our backs.
The stones were still aglow from the last fire
We didn't use them to warm our hands
Not with our own and not with other's ashes
The last smoke still hung gray under the stars
It didn't curtain off the future for us
Since other skies were under our eyelids
We saw with our eyes what had been written
With Marx' and Lenin's texts on our bodies
Not washed off in the quarry by our sweat
And not by our blood when we were tortured
Each of the two an Atlas of the new world
Where bread doesn't pull its square root from
Its eaters be they black or white or yellow
Since no one fills his stomach then with fear that
His bread will rip his guts out the next day
And no one tears into his fellow man
As soon as he takes bread between his teeth.

TRACTORIST:
If I show you my stump, what do you see.
(*Pause. Tractorist laughs.*)
And if you preach until your lips are shredded:
My stump is still the center of the world.
(*Pause.*)
You didn't bring a smoke for me, did you.
I haven't seen a beer for two weeks now.
I have forgotten what that is: a beer.

Always pushing the same stone up the same mountain. The stone's weight increasing, the toiler's strength decreasing with the ascent. Stalemate before the summit. A race against the stone which trundles down hill four times as fast as the toiler pushed it uphill. The stone's weight relatively increasing, the toiler's strength relatively decreasing with the ascent. The stone's weight absolutely decreasing with each uphill move, faster with each downhill move. The toiler's strength absolutely increasing with each operation (pushing the stone uphill, running downhill before beside behind the stone). Hope and disappointment. The rounding of the stone. The mutual attrition of man stone mountain. Until the imagined climax: The release of the stone from the attained summit into the abyss on the other side. Or until the feared point when the strength expires before the summit is within reach. Or until the conceivable point zero: no one moves nothing on a plane. STONE SCISSORS PAPER. STONE SHARPENS THE SCISSORS SCISSORS CUT THE PAPER PAPER WRAPS THE STONE.

HUNGER ARTIST

DOCTOR: We've patched you up, you can go and get torn again.
TRACTORIST: Are you a hunger artist. What do you want. I could just as well have been lucky and what happened to me had happened to someone else. One leg is better than no leg, everyone is doing his own work, one hero spares the next one, and anything could happen to anyone if he merely crosses the street, heads or tails. A man is not a machine. If at every handshake everyone wants to know what it will yield, we better twiddle our thumbs

and wait till grass grows from our bellies.
DOCTOR: Yes. See you again in my operating room.

According to Empedocles, first single limbs came up everywhere from the earth as if it were pregnant, then they grew together and formed the matter of a whole human being who is equally mixed of fire and water. "Well then, listen to how the purging fire made the sprouts of men and lamentable women who had been wrapped in darkness appear. First there came forth lumps of earth, still crude. They didn't show yet the lovely shape of the limbs, nor a voice or a penis. Heads without necks, arms roaming about by themselves without shoulders, and eyes roving alone, lacking their foreheads. Beings with paralyzed feet, yet having countless hands." And whatever joined together in such a way that it had the potential to survive, became living beings that stayed alive because they satisfied each other's needs such as that the teeth cut and chewed the food, the stomach digested it, the liver processed it so it became their blood. And if a head joined a body thus composed, the whole creature stayed alive, but it wouldn't fit a cow's trunk and then it perished. "Many creatures thus grew up with a double face or a two-fold breast, with the trunk of a cow but the face of a man, and conversely others appeared, men's bodies with cow's heads. Mongrel beings that had partly a man's, partly a woman's shape, furnished with indistinct genitals. Thus the sweet grabbed for the sweet, the bitter assaulted the bitter, the sour the sour, the warm poured itself unto the warm." Quite like Empedocles claimed that under the rule of love—as accident would have it—first parts of living beings, like heads, hands, and feet, were created and only then they joined each other. Wherever all parts came together as if they were aimed at a specific purpose, those beings survived since they had joined together accidentally in a way that fit. But all that didn't thus join perished or will perish.[7]

The liberation of the dead happens in slow motion.

THE HERO INVENTS A METHOD THAT RENDERS HEROES UNNECESSARY. PLOWING IN FORMATION.

(*Field.*)

YOUNG TRACTORIST: You can break your neck any place if that's what you want.
TRACTORIST: I can do it better here, I've learned it here.
YOUNG TRACTORIST: You've done your thing, now it's our turn. What's your doctor's name.
TRACTORIST: Stop.

"We take two tractors, attach the plow to a long rope and pull it behind us. The other one pulls it back again. That way we don't need to enter the dangerous field. If there are more of those things lying around, they only tear the plow apart, but we still must do the field." . . . Paul A. was also the first tractorist who formed brigades for plowing. The so-called *"plowing-in-formation"* was especially necessary on mined fields. The help of the partner was always needed, whether for repairs or in case explosions occurred. Often, a machine sagged into a filled-in trench. Then the second one drove over and tried to pull it out; that one sagged down, too. It was good, then, to have a third one around which pulled them both out.[8]

Either you ride the tractor or you're underneath it.[9]

AND WHEN THE BATTLE HAD BEEN LOST
THEY ALL WENT HOME THE BATTLEFIELD IN THEIR BREAST
AND MANY OF THEM STILL WERE FELLED
BOTH WEAPON AND AN ENEMY TO THEMSELVES.
AND MANY WON WHO WERE ALREADY GONE
LIKE GRASS FROM CORPSES GROWS IN SPRING

(*Night. Field. Tractorist. Farmer.*)

TRACTORIST:
   On your beet field—a cow would piss across—
   Even a nag is wasted. With my tractor
   I drive around it within sixty seconds.
   It isn't me. The tractor needs its space.
   Your beets, man, strangle it, they make it sick,
   Have you no feeling for a motor, friend?

If it breaks down, I don't care for your field
I do my nine-to-five day at the tavern
And when I'm drunk it's you who paid for it.
It was a night like this, a full moon too
When we snuffed out a guy in Russia
Three of us, on a corn field as large as
The state of Saxony. A farmer. Why?
I don't remember. What I do remember
Is: how the old guy on his last run still
Watched that he wouldn't tread the corn. We didn't
Watch. We chased him, and the chase was short
He kept dodging the corn, we stepped right on it.
And we had booze, the captain in high spirits
Said: Tell this Bolshevik because I like
His beard, I shall give him permission to
Dig his final hole on his own field.
We asked him where his field is. Said the old guy:
Hereisallmyfield. We: Where his field was when
It wasn't a collective. He just pointed
Like he was landed gentry all around where
For miles breast high the corn was standing tall.
He simply had forgotten where his field was.

Sources:

1. Pu Sung Ling
2. Helden der Arbeit (*Heroes of Labor*). Berlin, 1951
3. Po Chue Yi
4. Helden der Arbeit
5. Lenin
6. Dziga Vertov
7. Die Vorsokratiker (*The Pre-Socratics*). Ed. by W. Capelle. Berlin, 1961
8. Helden der Arbeit
9. Ernst Thalmann

LESSONS

LESSONS (*Lektionen*) is the title Heiner Müller gave to several short collections of poems published in the *Rotbuch* edition of his writings. The two sets of poems included here are selected from three of these volumes.

LESSON was written in the early fifties; TWO LETTERS in 1956, after the XXth Party Congress in Moscow with its revelations about Stalin's abuses of power; FILM in 1963, after the Wall had split the city of Berlin. The poems reflect on the artist's task and dilemma in the new age of Socialism, and on art's reception by an audience entrapped by old habits of living and viewing.

(Note: The *Magazin* referred to in TWO LETTERS was a popular monthly of the GDR, the first to publish photos of women in the nude. "Keuner's design" is a reference to a collection of anecdotes, *Stories of Mr. Keuner*, by Brecht. Johannes R. Becher was a major poet of German Expressionism; Brecht staged Becher's play *Winterschlacht* (Winter Battle) in 1955. At the time of Müller's poem, Becher was the Minister of Culture of the GDR.)

TALES OF HOMER was written in the early fifties, a comment on the "difficulties in writing the truth," to quote Brecht's title for one of his essays written in exile. OEDIPUS COMMENTARY, written in 1966, was intended as a prologue for the first production of Müller's adaptation of Sophocles' *Oedipus Tyrant*, January 31, 1967, directed by Benno Besson at Deutsches Theater, East Berlin. It was eventually only published in the production's playbill. Both texts are examples of Müller's continued investigation and revisioning of the classic Greek tradition of Western culture and thought, also evident in other texts of this volume.

C. W.

LESSON

In the traitor's book I read
About the loyalty of Communists
In Karaganda.

TWO LETTERS

1

I see you, sweating at your typewriter
Produce verses that can be misused
About death by asphyxia in the network
Of necessary laws. Bricklayers, you write
Have already been used as mortar
When the Great Wall was built and still
Great Walls are built. There's nothing new
Under the Sun, you write. You write nothing new.
You have learned to question all answers
Is the applause that's deafening you none?
The quick results are not the new ones.
An encounter at night after our conversation:

Two Citizens on their way to bed
Discuss democracy.
They count the years by their salary rises
The months by the issues of MAGAZIN
Each one a sage after Keuner's design
Not one thought that won't pass their stomach first
Small brains, but they are right
If, reading your verses, they say:
What is this somebody trying to tell us?
Hasn't he understood the function of agrarian reform?

2

What can a rhyme do against blockheads
You're asking. Nothing, some people say, others say: Little.
Shakespeare has written *Hamlet,* a tragedy
Story of a man who threw away what he knew
Submitting to a foolish custom.
He didn't exterminate folly.
Did he only try to write a warrant?
Hamlet the Dane Prince and maggot's fodder
Stumbling from hole to hole towards the final
Hole listless In his back the ghost that once
Made him Green like Ophelia's flesh in childbed
The horizon The armor will last longer
And shortly ere the third cock's crow a clown
Will tear the fool's cap off the philosopher
A bloated bloodhound he'll crawl into the armor.
Or Bertolt Brecht who was misunderstood
With great tenacity and some hope
He, too, couldn't do more than bend the bow
How many blockheads have survived the man.
Becher has shed his sweat constructing sonnets
To join the Volga with the Neckar River.
The farmers of the Jura, will they have
Studied the poet's works when Communism
Lifts the farmland's burden from their backs?
Our's the margin between Naught and Little.

FILM

45 years after the Great
Revolution I see on the screen
In a new film from the country of Soviets the transformation
Of a tardy waiter into a sprinter
Through the false report the hundred-and-first
Customer waiting was a State Prize Winner.
The spectators, more or less dressed alike
In the small moviehouse in the split capital
Of my split fatherland, laugh at
The everyday occurence, not everyday
On the screen. Why did these people laugh.
O tardiness of those who aren't any more driven
Never enough to be praised! Beautiful unkindness
Of those no one can force any more to smile!

HERACLES 5

HERACLES 5 was written in 1964-66. It was published in the volume *Philoktet. Heracles 5* (Edition Suhrkamp # 163), Frankfurt, 1966. The first production was directed by Ernst Wendt and opened June 9, 1974, at the Schiller Theater, West Berlin; the play appeared at East Berlin's Volksbühne a few months later, September 25, 1974, in the staging of Thomas Vallentin. There were soon a few more productions in West Germany and Switzerland but since then the play has been rarely performed, undeservedly so. (In the U.S., there was, to my knowledge, only a staged reading of an earlier translation by Martin W. Walsh, at the Brecht Company, Residential College, University of Michigan, Ann Arbor.)

HERACLES 5 is one of the two outright comedies Müller has published, the other being WOMEN'S COMEDY (*Weiberkomödie*), 1971, which was based on a radio play by his first wife Inge, *Die Weiberbrigade.*

HERACLES 5 satirizes the need—or rather, the craving—for a hero but also the hero's ambiguous position: much needed, he also is little liked and eventually has to reap his rewards by force. And while lip service is payed to his "greatness," he is snickered at by those who beg for his help. The text directs its barbs as much at the hero and his gargantuan appetites as at those who clamor for him. What twenty-five years ago was undoubtedly understood as a laughing reflection on the cult of "great leaders," could today be read in the context of popular culture which idolizes, devours, and discards its "heroes" at an ever-increasing pace. The play also satirizes a stance officially taken during the 50s and 60s in the GDR which tried to glamorize even the least attractive forms of manual labor by painting them as heroic achievements. Müller shows such labor for what it really is; he supports the rebellion against it, and its elimination by inventive technologies.

Written at a time when Müller was investigating and elaborating Brecht's *Lehrstück* model, that form is quite visible in the lighthearted play which also reflects the work on Greek drama and mythology he did for adaptations of tragedies by Aeschylus and

Sophocles during the sixties. In its bold images and amusing contempt for practicalites of the stage, playful tossing about of theatrical convention, and its challenge to any director's imagination, the text anticipates a theatre of imagery and fragmentation the author didn't fully explore until 1972. Then his play CEMENT presented an early example of his experimentation with the ''synthetic fragment''; one of the play's interludes is called HERACLES 2 OR THE HYDRA.

C. W.

Wilfried Hösl

HERACLES 5
Bayerisches Staatsschauspiel, Munich, 1985.
Director: B. K. Tragelehn.

CHARACTERS: Heracles, Augias, Zeus, Two Thebans

1

(*Heracles asleep in the midst of cattle skeletons; he's holding one in his hand, snores. Voices call: Heracles. Two Thebans enter. They're holding their noses.*)

FIRST: Again. He's gorged up to his gullet.
SECOND: Softly.
FIRST: (*More softly with increased anger.*)
   After each labor it is one ox more!
SECOND: Would you then like to do the job?
FIRST: Would you?
SECOND: The paean.
FIRST: (*Terrified.*)   All its stanzas?
SECOND: (*Indignant.*)   Without nose?
BOTH:
   He who strangled the Hydra
   (*Both shake their heads.*)
   Beheaded
   (*Both nod.*)
      the Nemean Lion
   (*Both shake their heads.*)

He who has strangled the Nemean Lion and beheaded the Hydra
He who has captured the hind and the boar, destroyer of harvests
(*Heracles yawns.*)
Heracles, son of Alcmene, sired in Amphitryon's bed
(*They grin.*)
Not by Amphitryon—
(*Thunder. The Thebans spit into each other's face.*)
Swine, you're insulting the Gods!
(*Louder.*) Heracles, son of Amphitryon, lend us
You doer of four great deeds, your arm for the fifth one
And deign to cleanse the stable of Augias. Oh, liberator
Liberate us from the stench of this fleshpot regrettably needed.
(*Heracles holds his nose.*)
FIRST: We count your oxen as we count the labors.
SECOND: It will be the fifth labor.
FIRST: Makes five oxen.
HERACLES: Liberate yourselves. (*Snores.*)
BOTH: You're Heracles.
HERACLES: (*Gets up, vainglorious.*)
   I'll liberate your Thebes then from its stench.
   And my advance . . .
   (*Roaring of an ox who's butchered.*)
THEBANS: You hear it roaring, don't you.
   (*The ox is brought in.*)
HERACLES: (*Sits down.*)
   You're dismissed.
THEBANS: And rush the job, please. Thebes
   Needs our arm.
   (*Backdrop: Thebes in ruins, the populace in rags.*)
HERACLES: And me. Get off my table.
   (*Thebans exeunt. Heracles eats the ox.*)

2

(*Augias' stable, right and left a river. Enter Heracles. He holds his nose.*)

HERACLES: Augias! (*Enter Augias.*)
AUGIAS: Heracles. What do you want?
HERACLES: Clean your stable.

AUGIAS: With one hand?

(*Heracles takes his hand off his nose, collapses, Augias laughs, Heracles holds his nose again, gets up.*)

My beef is good for your bellies, your noses are too fine for its muck. And even if the plague is stinking from my stable: are you immortal without the plague? The end lives in the beginning, the dead in the loins. What do you have against manure? How long does it stink? Open your nostrils. Three days and you can't breathe without the stench that burst your nose on the first day. The muck is rising, the stench increasing. Not for you, you live in it. Your fifth labor?

(*Heracles counts his fingers, nods.*)

Did you know Sisyphus? Do you hear my cows shitting?

(*Music.*)

And no end to it. Number six is canceled. Feces are the other condition of the flesh. And its last shape. No exit from the shitting community but to the democracy of the dead. Two rivers. Take your pick. A river swallows it all, flesh or manure makes no difference, and out to sea. A bucket, a shovel.

(*From the flies: a bucket, a shovel.*)

You can have two shovels. You won't be able to handle more than one, with two hands at a time. Two shovels aren't more than one, two thousand won't be more, with all that muck. And my cows are shitting fast, you hear it.

(*Music.*)

You won't finish one way or another: you can use the handle for dredging. And don't you hope that the wood will sprout leaves and cover itself with foliage, flip-flop back into the tree against the root, muck turns into grass on its way back through the flesh, andsoforth, because your father lives one heaven above us. Or use your hands, if you like: ten prongs. How did you slaughter the sea-wolf at Crete? A dive from the cliff through its jaws into its belly and back through its flesh with the knife. Here's your towering cliff, your gleaming knife, your stinking fish.

(*Augias exits. Heracles shovels and hauls manure, first with one hand, the other holding his nose, then with both hands.*)

HERACLES: Oh, envied Sisyphus, his stone rolling odorless.

Oh, happy water, it has no nose. Father, thou maker of all flesh, why does your flesh shit?

(*Throws bucket and shovel down, takes his bow.*)

Stench, where are you? Come out of your monstrous shape, show your ugly mug. Is your dwelling the void of nothingness? I will lard it with arrows. And if you're everywhere, I'll hit you everywhere.

(*Shoots wildly in all directions, throws the bow down and takes his club.*)

We're enemies, dung. Go voluntarily into the river of your choice. The river or the club.

(*Waits for the effect. No effect.*)

You've made your choice.

(*Slams the club into the muck, howls in pain, blinded by the muck. Laughter of Augias.*)

I'll laugh after you.

(*To the cattle:*)

                  Out of your stable.
Come and wash your feces from my face.
You ate the grass. Now also eat what you
Have made from grass. The earth sustains you and
You shit on it in gratitude. Now eat or
I'm your stable and your grave my belly.

(*Protest from Thebes.*)

You're lucky, beef. Thebes doesn't want to eat grass.

(*He picks up the shovel again.*)

And I won't eat manure!

(*He throws the shovel down again.*)

Hear me, Thebans! See my weakness and release me from your labor which was too great for me. Look at my arms, not strong enough to lift this tool.

(*He demonstrates that he cannot lift the shovel.*)

Look at my legs which barely are supporting me.

(*He falls down. Applause and laughter from Thebes. Voices: Bravo. What an act. Hurrah for Heracles. Da Capo.*)

Who's Heracles? I, body without a name. I, dunghill without a face.

(*Increasing applause. Voices: Look at his mask! That's what I call style! Heracles, on his hands and knees, hides under his lion's skin, roars.*)

I've eaten him, your Heracles. He's lost his way in the maze of my guts. Through the fence of my teeth his last word was uttered. I'm the Nemean Lion. There is room for three Thebes in my belly.

(*Increasing applause. Voices: He doesn't act the lion, he is the lion. I can't stop laughing. My husband laughed till he dropped dead. That's the art of acting. Nice art: I have four children. Stop it. Go on. Murderer. Enough. Da Capo. Stop it. Go on. Enough. Da Capo.*)

Yeaaaaaaaaaaaaaaaaaaaaaaaaaaaaaaaaaaaaaaaaaaaaaaaaaaaaaaaaaaaah! The dunghill, that's me; the voice from the feces is my voice, under that mask of feces, that's my face. That's what his fifth labor made of Heracles, the doer of your deeds. Would I hadn't done the first one! I wouldn't stand in this my fifth one, stinking, my fame my prison, with each deed snared into the next one, with each freedom harnessed to a new yoke, a victor conquered by his victories, Heracles forced into Heracles. Willingly you've fed women to the Hydra, deaf to their last screams while you expected your own last scream when the lion was devouring the men. I've strangled the lion, I returned, more a wound than flesh, in its bloody skin, and you wanted to keep your women. I cut off the Hydra's heads for nine long days, sealed the necks with fire, the remains to the dogs, I returned on my hands and knees, breathless, to your Thebes that breathed a sigh of relief, and the small evils were colossal. They're gone, now you want your beef without the muck. I reduced your death by four of its shapes, now you want life without its last one, the murder of the new tomorrow: Immortality. I'll take back all my deeds. Time shall stop. Roll backwards, Time. Crawl back into your skin, Nemean Lion. Hydra, grow your heads back again. Andsoforth.

(*Applause from Thebes. Voices: Hear, hear, how he thinks. That's what I call Dialectics. Heracles the Thinker. Heracles hurls muck into the audience. Frenetic applause. Voices: Look how he's working. Heracles the Working Man. Go back to your houses, don't disturb his work.*)

Watch, Thebans, what I'm going to do now
With Heracles, the doer of your deeds:
I'll throw him in the muck, the muck his grave
And rising it will bury you and Thebes.

(*Heracles goes into position to jump into the muck. Vomiting.*)

What's Thebes to me, and who are you then? I
Am nobody, nobody's son who hasn't
Done a thing.

(*Zeus on a cloud. He holds his nose.*)

ZEUS: Do your job now, Heracles, my son.
HERACLES: Why me, father?
ZEUS: Here is your reward.

(*He beckons. On another cloud, Hebe sails by. She is nude and also holding her nose.*)

HERACLES: Stay! Those breasts! And what a pair of thighs!
   Surrender, muck, Heracles is himself again.
   Did I say you stink, burden who supports me?
   See my fist, it hits the slanderer.
   (*Hits himself on the nose.*)
   Beauty of labor, fragrance of the muck
   I am anticipating blissful luck!
   (*Enter a jealous bull.*)
   Welcome in heat! What do you want? It's not
   Your cows my third leg's getting up for.
   My heaven grazes on another meadow.
   You've got one horn too many?
   (*The bull attacks.*)
                             Sure.
(*Bullfight. Heracles is victorious and harnesses the bull to the bucket.*)
                             Pull!
(*The bull does so and falls into the river.*)
                             Halt!
(*Heracles pulls the bucket and with it the bull from the river.*)
You've got to earn your death, now do your job.
Pull, Heracles!
(*The bull doesn't move.*)
                  Your pay: five pecks of grass.
(*The bull pulls.*)
And a cow your heaven.
(*The bull pulls faster.*)
                   That quickens him.—

Fill the bucket, too, and empty it.

Do all the work if you want all your pay.

(*The bull tries dredging the muck, the muck spills on Heracles instead of into the bucket.*)

Oh mirror most imperfect! Half-baked toy!

If you won't be complete, be nothing then.

(*Heracles hurls the bull into the river. With the bull goes the bucket.*)

AUGIAS: My bull! You'll pay for him.

HERACLES: River, my bull!

Keep the bull but spit back the bucket. Would you like to wash the stable? You can forget the ocean. Your banks will devour you. My cows will fill you with shit. Your banks will devour you with the assholes of my cows. My cows will shit you full with the jaws of your banks.

AUGIAS: Did I hear you say: my cows?

HERACLES: And your muck.

(*Throws the shovel down. Protest from Thebes.*)

I shit on Thebes.

(*Hear, Hear! and jeers from Thebes. Hebe sails by on her cloud. Heracles picks up the shovel again.*)

                                 For Thebes. River, the bucket!

Augias. A bucket.

AUGIAS: First my bull.

HERACLES: My father on your cloud, step forward here

And tell your river: Lend my son an ear.

(*Silence.*)

Who's more to you, your river or your son?

Hear what I want, tell him what's to be done.

(*Silence.*)

Your silence, dad, is smacking of my sweat.

(*Zeus on his cloud, in his arms a nude woman, etc.*)

ZEUS: Do your job. Without sweat no prize yet.

(*He's gone.*)

HERACLES: Did you say work? Gulp down the shovel, too.

(*Throws the shovel into the river.*)

Be what you robbed me of, river: my bucket

River: my shovel and my bull. You on the

Left there, too. Two will wash more than one.
If you can't hear me, listen to my fist
I'll tame you and I'll change your course and tame
You too, your course will change if my fist speaks.
(*To the above.*)
Watch out, what I'll do with your water, dad.
You didn't help me, now observe how I
Will help myself and what your river can do
When he must do it since he's yoked by me.
(*Struggles with the river.*)
River, have you no body then but none?
River, have you no other weight but mine?
Who are you, foe and battleground in one
Who armed with myself is now wrestling me?
There's no neck yet I didn't harness, but
Your river has no neck to throw my yoke on.
(*A cow steps to the riverbank, drinks and pisses.*)
Thanks for your model. How to steer a river.
(*Drinks.*)
I am your mouth.
(*Pisses.*)
              I am your source as well.
Now do my work and wash the stable.
You're getting lost in the intestine's maze?
Where is your stride that in its torrent canceled
My strength with your strength of a thousand bulls?
And now you're mocking me with this your weakness
That won't move even one small speck of dust
Deaf to my words and deaf to all my strength
Nothing but silt that clogs my body's engine.
What's left? Hand, you're my shovel; hand, my bucket.
And Heracles is Heracles my bull.
(*Manual labor.*)
I'd rather move the world than its manure!
(*Building a dike.*)
Look: your mountain's walking with my legs.
Look: your river's rising at your mountainside.
(*Thunder.*)
Did I forget to ask you? Permit me to change your world, Papa.

Augias, drive your cattle from your stable
I'm coming, Heracles, two rivers strong
Lord of the waters and your stableboy
The river is my hand and is my strength
He who was conquered by my hand
He who was conquerred by my weakness.

AUGIAS: My stable! My cattle!

SHOUTS FROM THEBES: Our beef to the fish!

HERACLES: (*Opens the dam.*)

Out of my way, you cattlebaron. Here
I come and wash your stable, Heracles
The river, steered by Heracles, the pilot
Of the rivers.
(*Thunder.*)
                    I know that you can thunder.
And I can steer your rivers, look, unbridled,
     wherever I like to.
(*Winter. The river stops in its tracks, frozen.*)
Hey, what's that supposed to mean?

AUGIAS: Heracles, the pilot of rivers.

HERACLES: (*To the above.*)
You've started it.
(*Rips the sun from the sky, holds it in his hand until the ice melts.
Hand and stable are burning.*)
Where's your winter, Zeus?

AUGIAS: My stable's burning.

HERACLES: (*Looks at his hand, it is black.*)
                                        Does it?

Not for long. Make way, Augias.
(*The river washes the stable.*)

AUGIAS: Seven oxen!

(*Rejoicing from Thebes. Shouts: Long live Heracles! Bravo. Da
Capo. Heracles whistles mountain and rivers back to their places.*)

HERACLES: The job is done. And now: Where's my reward?

(*Thunder and lightning.*)

AUGIAS: Why don't you ask my cows for your reward.
     See you again in your muck of tomorrow.

HERACLES: Did I hear you say: My cows?
AUGIAS: And your muck.
HERACLES: My river will take care of your muck gratis.
   Your stable and your cattle, they are mine.
   Now, play your final scene.
   (*He rips Augias in two and throws the halves into the river, pulls
   down the sky, reaches for Hebe. Before the wedding, two
   Thebans enter.*)
THEBANS: He who strangled the Nemean Lion and beheaded the
   Hydra
   He who captured the hind and the boar, destroyer of harvests
   He who cleaned the stable of Augias, stinking fleshpot
   Heracles, son of Alcmene, sired in Amphitryon's bed.
   (*They grin.*)
   Not by Amphitryon—
   (*They dodge. Silence.*)
                              Not by Amphitryon—
   (*They shout.*)
                                 Not by Amphitryon!
   Doer of five great deeds. Lend us your arm for the sixth one.

(*Heracles rolls up the sky and puts it in his pocket.*)

                                                      1964

LESSONS 2

TALES OF HOMER

1

Often and in abundance his pupils were talking with Homer
Elucidating his work and demanding correct explanation.
Because the old poet loved to discover himself afresh
And when extolled wasn't stingy with wine and a roast.
During a feast, the meat and the wine, the talk once turned to
Thersites, the much despised one, the gossip, who rose in assembly
Cleverly using the war lord's quarrel for the size of their spoils
Said he: Look at the people's shepherd who is shearing and killing
Like any shepherd does with his sheep, and he showed the bloody
Empty hands of the soldiers to the soldiers as empty and bloody.
And then the pupils asked: How is that with this Thersites
Master? You let him say the right words but then with your own
    words
You prove him wrong. This seems to be difficult to understand.
Why did you do it? Said the old man: To be liked by the princes.
Asked his pupils: Why that? The old man: From hunger. For
    laurels?
Too. But he liked it as much in his fleshpot as on his head.

2

One of the pupils, however, they say was uniquely bright
A great one for questions. He always questioned each answer he got
In his search for the one, the definitive answer. He asked

Sitting at the riverside with the old man the question again
As once the others. The old man looked at the youngster and said
Calmly: Truth is an arrow, poisoned to all hasty archers!
Even bending the bow is much. The arrow will still be an
Arrow if found among rushes. Truth dressed as a lie is still truth.
And the bow won't die with the archer. Said it and rose.

OEDIPUS COMMENTARY

Laius was King in Thebes. The god told him from the mouth of
Priests his son would walk over him. Laius, unwilling
To pay the price of a birth that would cost him his life, he tore
From the breasts of the mother the new one and pierced his toes
Carefully sewing them up threefold so he wouldn't walk over him.
Gave him so that he would serve him to birds on a table of
    mountains
To an old servant: *this my own flesh won't overgrow me.*
And so he spread by his caution the foot which trampled on him:
To the winged hunger the servant refused to offer the child
Gave it to other hands so they would take it to other countries
There the highborn grew up on his misshapen swollen feet
Nobody walks like me: his blemish his name, on his feet
And on others', fate took his course, resistible every
Step but the next one irresistible, one step took the other.
Look at the poem of Oedipus, Laius' son from Jocasta
Unbeknowst to himself, in Thebes a tyrant through merit:
He solved since he couldn't flee on his crippled foot the riddle
Posed by the three times born Sphinx, a terror to the city of Thebes
Offered to eat to the stone the threeheaded man-eating monster
And Man was the solution. For years in a happy city
Plowed he the bed once conceived in, a lucky bringer of luck.
Longer than good luck is time, and longer than bad luck: The tenth
Year of his rule, the plague fell from the unknown on the city
Many years happy. And bodies it broke and the order of things.
Ringed by his ruled, the new riddle heavily crushing his shoulders
Stood he on his too big foot, the cries of the dying around him
Solver of riddles, he threw into darkness his questions like nets:
Is the messenger lying, sent to the priests, mouth of gods?

Does the blind man who points his ten fingers at him speak the
    truth?
Out of the darkness the nets bounce back, and there in their meshes
On his own tracks overtaken by his own steps: he.
And his low point is his peak: he overtook time itself
Caught in a circle, *I and no end,* he caught: himself.
In his eyesockets he buries the world. Was there once a tree?
Is there still flesh outside of his own? None, and no trees
With voices his ear is talking to him, the ground is his thought
Mud or stone, as his foot is thinking, and from his hands
Sometimes a wall grows, *the world is a wart,* or his finger creates
Him once again in intercourse with the air until he
Wipes out the image himself with his hand. And so he lives
Being his own grave, regurgitating and chewing his dead.
See his example, he who jumped from a bloodied start
In the freedom of Man caught by the teeth of Man
On feet far too few, with not enough hands he grasps at space.

THE HORATIAN

THE HORATIAN (*Der Horatier*) was written in 1968. It wasn't professionally performed until five years later when Ernst Wendt's production opened at the Schiller Theater, West Berlin, on March 1, 1973. A first printing appeared in the playbill for the production, *Programm des Schiller Theater's der Staatlichen Schauspielbühnen Berlin*, # 14/1973. Published translations include those in English, by Helen Fehervary, Marc Silberman, and Guntram Weber, in *Minnesota Review*, NS 6/Spring 1976, and in French in *Hamletmachine*, translated by Jean Jourdheuil and Heinz Schwarzinger, Paris, 1979. It was included in an anthology *Sozialistiches Drama nach Brecht*, Darmstadt-Neuwied, 1974; in the collection *Heiner Müller: Stücke,* East Berlin, 1975; and in Volume 6 of the Rotbuch edition, *Mauser*, West Berlin, 1978. Müller himself directed the text in January 1988, when he inserted it in the first scene of his production of *The Scab*, at Deutsches Theater, East Berlin.

THE HORATIAN is the second in a sequence of *Lehrstücke* (didactic plays) which Müller wrote between 1958 and 1970; the first being PHILOCTETES, the last MAUSER. It refers to the same Roman legend on which Brecht based his *Lehrstück* THE HORATIANS AND THE CURIATIANS (1933/34), conceived for performance by children or young adolescents. Müller tells a story completely different from Brecht's though he follows closely the *Lehrstück* model, a genre Brecht defined as "plays that are didactic for the performers. They actually don't need an audience." Thus, it was thoroughly consistent when Müller welcomed the plan of a young amateur group, the "Billstedt Students and Apprentices Theater" of Hamburg, to work on a production of the play in 1972. The young performers had some difficulty with the text and decided to incorporate introductions to each segment/scene to bring the story closer to their own and their audiences' experiences. Müller, though not in full agreement with each and every one of their changes, approved their decision in a letter: "Once again, I agree—as I said earlier—that you furnish from the text something which fits your own perceptions. We needn't have discussed this so much if I'd seen how you did it. That our opinions differ about the means towards our mutually agreed upon end is understandable, if only because of 'geographic' reasons, of course." In other words, Müller viewed his text as a blueprint which could be adapted to different conditions if such a procedure supported its didactic purpose.

After MAUSER had been performed, and while PHILOCTETES had achieved general acclaim and become quite a "commercial" success, Müller stated in a letter to Reiner Steinweg, the foremost theoretician of the *Lehrstück*: ". . . I think we have to say 'goodbye' to the *Lehrstück* until the next earthquake . . . In a landscape where the TEACHINGS are buried so deeply, and which is riddled with mines to boot, one must at times push his head into the sand (mud, rock) to look farther. The moles, or constructive defeatism." (January 4, 1977)

The next earthquake is approaching in Müller's judgment: With VOLOKOLAMSK HIGHWAY he has returned to the *Lehrstück* and resumed his experimentation with its form and intentions.

C. W.

Sibylle Bergemann

THE HORATIAN
Deutsches Theater, East Berlin, 1988. Director: Heiner Müller.
As prologue to THE SCAB.

Between the city of Rome and the city of Alba
There was a contest for dominance. Against the contestants
Stood the Etruscans' power, armed for war.
The cities, both threatened, assembled facing each other
In battle array to settle their contest
Before the expected assault. The commanders-in-chief
Stepped each one in front of their armies and said
One to the other: Since a battle will weaken
Conqueror and conquered, let us cast lots
So that one man will fight for our city
Against one who fights for the city of yours
Sparing all others for our mutual foe
And the armies rapped with their swords on their shields
Expressing agreement and then the lots were cast.
The lots determined to fight
For Rome a Horatian, for Alba a Curiatian.
The Curiatian was betrothed to the Horatian's sister
And the Horatian and the Curiatian
Were asked, each one by his army:

He is   your
        betrothed to   sister
You are   his
Shall the lot

Be cast one more time?
And the Horatian and the Curiatian said: No
And they fought between the lines of battle
And the Horatian wounded the Curiatian
And the Curiatian said with his voice on the wane:
Spare the conquered man. I am
Betrothed to your sister.
And the Horatian yelled:
My bride's name is Rome
And the Horatian thrust his sword into
The Curiatian's throat so that his blood dropped to the earth.
When the Horatian came home to the city of Rome
Carried high on the shields of the unharmed army
Draped on his shoulder the warrior's mantle of
The Curiatian whom he had killed in combat
At his belt the captured sword, in his hands his own, dripping with
    blood
There came towards him at the Eastern gate of the city
With quick strides his sister and behind her
His old father, slowly
And the conqueror leapt from the shields, the crowd rejoicing,
And raised his arms to accept the embrace of his sister.
But the sister recognized the bloodied mantle
Work of her hands, and wailed and let her hair down.
And the Horatian scolded the mourning sister:
Why do you wail and let down your hair.
Rome has conquered. The conqueror stands before you.
And the sister kissed the bloodied mantle and screamed:
Rome.
Give back to me what was clothed in this mantle.
And the Horatian—his arm still felt the sword's thrust
He had killed the Curiatian with in combat,
The man he saw his sister weeping for now—
Thrust the sword—the blood of the man she wept for
Wasn't yet dry on it—
Into the breast of the weeping girl
So that her blood dropped to the earth. He said:
Go join him, whom you love more than Rome.
That much for each Roman woman

Who bemoans our foe.
And he showed the twice bloodied sword to all Romans
And the rejoicing was silenced. Only back in
The onlooking crowd still some shouting was heard:
Hail to the hero. There, they hadn't yet noticed
The horror. When in the silent crowd the father
Had arrived where his children were
He had only one child left. He said:
You have killed your sister.
And the Horatian didn't hide his twice bloodied sword
And the Horatian's father
Looked at the twice bloodied sword and said:
You have conquered. Rome
Is ruling Alba.
He wept for his daughter, hiding his face
Covered her wound with the warrior's mantle
Work of her hands, bloodied by the same sword
And embraced the conqueror.
To the Horatians, now
The lictors stepped, with bundle of rods and ax they parted
The embrace, took the captured sword
From the conqueror's belt and from the murderer's hand
His own one
Twice bloodied.
And one of the Romans shouted:
He has conquered. Rome
Is ruling Alba.
And another one of the Romans replied:
He has killed his sister.
And the Romans shouted against each other:
Honor the conqueror.
Try the murderer.
And Romans took up the sword against Romans in quarrel
If as a conqueror he should be honored
Or as a murderer tried, the Horatian.
The lictors
Parted the quarreling parties with bundle of rods and ax
And called to assembly the people
And the people appointed out of their midst two men

To pass judgment on the Horatian
And they put into the hand of one
The conqueror's laurel
And into the other's the ax, fate of the murderer
And the Horatian stood
Between laurel and ax.
But his father stepped to his side
He who had lost most, and said:
Disgraceful sight, even the Albans wouldn't
Watch without shame.
The city is threatened by the Etruscans
And Rome is breaking her best sword.
You care for one.
Care for Rome.
And one of the Romans answered him:
Rome has many swords.
No Roman
Is less than Rome or there is no Rome.
And another one of the Romans said
And pointed his finger where the enemy stood:
Twice powerful
Is the Etruscan if Rome is in strife
Split by opinion
At a trial ill-timed.
And the first one reasoned thus his opinion:
A dispute undisputed
Weakens the sword arm.
Discord disclaimed
Scatters the battle array.
And the lictors parted a second time
The Horatian's embrace, and the Romans took up their arms
Each one his own sword.
He, holding the laurel and he, holding the sword
Each one his own sword, so that their left hand now
Held laurel or sword and a sword was held by
The right hand. The lictors themselves
Laid down for one breath
The emblems of their office and put
Their swords into their belts, each one, and took

Up again bundle of rods and ax
And the Horatian stooped for
His sword, the bloodied one, that lay in the dust.
But the lictors
Restrained him with bundle of rods and ax.
And the Horatian's father took also his sword and went
To pick up with his left hand the bloodied sword
Of the conqueror who was a murderer
And the lictors restrained him too
And the guards were increased at the city's four gates
And the trial continued
While they expected the foe.
And the laurel bearer said:
His merit cancels his guilt
And the sword bearer said:
His guilt cancels his merit
And the laurel bearer asked:
Shall the conqueror be executed?
And the sword bearer asked:
Shall the murderer be honored?
And the laurel bearer said:
If the murderer is executed
The conqueror is executed.
And the sword bearer said:
If the conqueror is honored
The murderer is honored.
And the people looked at the one undivided
Doer of two different deeds and were silent.
And they who held laurel and sword, they asked:
If the one cannot be done
Without the other that will make it undone
                conqueror   murderer
Since   and   are one man, indivisible
           murderer   conqueror
Shall we then do none of the two
           conquest   conqueror
So there'll be a   but no
           murder   murderer
        conqueror

And the   will be called no one?
        murderer
And the people answered with one voice
(But the Horatian's father was silent):
There is the conqueror. His name: Horatius.
There is the murderer. His name: Horatius.
There are many men within one man.
One man has conquered for Rome in combat of swords.
Another one has murdered his sister
Without necessity. To each one his own.
To the conqueror the laurel, to the murderer the ax.
And the Horatian was crowned with the laurel
And the laurel bearer raised his sword
High to the sky and honored the conqueror
And the lictors stooped and laid down the
Bundle of rods and ax and picked up the sword
Twice bloodied with two kinds of blood
That lay in the dust and handed it to the conqueror
And the Horatian, his temple crowned with laurel
Raised his sword that it was seen by all
The one twice bloodied with two kinds of blood
And the ax bearer laid down the ax, and all Romans
Raised each one his sword for the time of three heartbeats
High to the sky and honored the conqueror.
And the lictors put back their swords
Into their belts and took the sword
Of the conqueror from the murderer's hand and threw it
Back into the dust again, and the ax bearer ripped
The laurel from the murderer's temple
The laurel that crowned the conqueror, and handed
It back to the laurel bearer and threw
Upon the Horatian's head a cloth as black as the night
Into which he was sentenced to go
Because he had killed a human being
Without necessity, and all the Romans
Each one of them, they sheathed their sword
That all the blades were covered from sight and thus
The arms they honored the conqueror with didn't share in
The murderer's execution. But the guards

At the four gates, expecting the enemy
They didn't cover their swords
And the blades of the axes also remained uncovered
And the conqueror's sword that lay in the dust, bloody.
And the Horatian's father said:
He is my last one. Kill me instead of him.
And the people answered with one voice:
No man is another man
And the Horatian was executed by the ax
So that his blood dropped to the earth
And the laurel bearer, in his hand
The conqueror's laurel again, torn badly
Because it was ripped off the murderer's temple
Asked the people:
What shall be done with the conqueror's corpse?
And the people answered with one voice:
The conqueror's corpse shall lay in state
On the shields of the army saved by his sword.
And they put together as well as they could
That which wasn't to be reconciled
The murderer's head and the murderer's body
Parted by the executioner's ax
Bleeding both on their own, as the conqueror's corpse
On the shields of the army saved by his sword
Not heeding his blood that was flowing over the shields
Not heeding his blood on their hands, and they placed
On his temple the badly torn laurel
And forced into his hand, its fingers still crooked
From the last cramp, his dust-covered bloody sword
And crossed their naked swords above him, pointing
Out that nothing was to harm the corpse
Of the Horatian who had conquered for Rome
Neither rain nor time, neither snow nor oblivion
And they covered their faces and mourned him.
But the guards at the four gates
Expecting the foe
Didn't cover their faces.
And the ax bearer, in his hands again the ax
The conqueror's blood on it not yet dry

Asked the people:
What shall be done with the murderer's corpse?
And the people answered with one voice:
(But the last of the Horatians was silent):
The murderer's corpse
Shall be thrown to the dogs
That they shall tear him to shreds
And nothing will remain of him
Who has killed a human being
Without necessity.
And the last Horatian, in his face
Two-fold the trace of tears, he said:
The conqueror is dead, never to be forgotten
As long as Rome will rule Alba.
Forget the murderer as I have forgotten him
The one who lost most.
And one of the Romans answered him:
Longer than Rome will rule Alba
Rome won't be forgotten and the example
That it once set or didn't set
Measuring with the merchant's balance
Or neatly sifting guilt and merit
Of the indivisible doer of different deeds
Afraid of the impure truth or not afraid
And half an example is no example
What isn't done fully to its true ending
Returns to nothing at the leash of time in a crab's walk.
And they took the laurel away from the conqueror
And one of the Romans bowed to the corpse
And said:
Permit that we force from your hand,
Conqueror who won't feel anything anymore
The sword which we need now.
Another one of the Romans spat on the corpse and said:
Murderer. surrender the sword.
And the sword was broken from his hand
Because his hand in rigor mortis
Had closed itself around the sword's hilt
They had to break the Horatian's fingers

To make him surrender the sword
He had killed with for Rome and once
Not for Rome, the sword bloodied once-too-many
So others put to better use what he
Had used well but once didn't use well.
And the murderer's corpse, by the ax divided
Was thrown to the dogs that they tear him apart
So nothing at all would remain of him
Who had killed a human being
Without necessity, or as much as nothing.
And one of the Romans asked the others:
What shall we call the Horatian for those after us?
And the people answered with one voice:
He shall be called the conqueror of Alba
He shall be called the murderer of his sister
Within one breath his merit and his guilt.
And whoever speaks of his guilt and not of his merit
Shall dwell where the dogs dwell, as a dog
And whoever speaks of his merit but not of his guilt
He, too, shall dwell among dogs.
But he who speaks of his guilt at one time
And at other times speaks of his merit
Differently speaking with one mouth at different times
Or differently to different ears
His tongue shall be torn from his mouth.
Since the words must be kept pure. Because
A sword may be broken and also a man
Maybe broken, but words
They fall into the wheels of the world, irretrievably
Making things known to us or unknown.
Deadly to humans is what they can't understand.
Thus, expecting their foe, they set—not afraid
Of the impure truth—a provisional example
Of neat distinction, and didn't hide the rest
That wasn't resolved in the unceasing change of things.
And each one went back to his work again, in his hand
Besides the plow, the hammer, the awl, or the style,
The sword.

Author's Note

The text is to be played according to its description.
(ALL PLAYERS: Between the city of Rome . . . the expected assault.
POSITIONS. THE COMMANDERS-IN-CHIEF: The commanders-in-chief / stepped each one in front of their armies and said// One to the other: Since a battle will weaken . . . etc. Variant: THE COMMANDERS-IN-CHIEF: The commanders-in-chief / stepped each one in front of their armies and said / One to the other. ALL PLAYERS: Since a battle will weaken . . .)

All Props: Masks (masks for the Romans and the Albanians, mask of the sister, dog masks), weapons, etc., are visible throughout the performance. No exits. Whoever has spoken his/her text and has performed his/her actions, returns to his/her original position, viz. changes his/her role. (The Albanians, after the combat, play the people of Rome who receive the conqueror. Two Roman soldiers, after the murder, play the lictors, etc.) After each killing, a player drops a red cloth downstage, near the footlights. The player of the Horatian can be replaced by a dummy after he has been killed. The dummy should be larger-than-life. The text: "Because his hand in rigor mortis . . ." is in any case to be spoken by the player of the Horatian.

H. M., 1968

MAUSER

MAUSER was written in 1970. It was first performed in English translation while Heiner Müller was Writer in Residence at the Department of German, University of Texas at Austin. The University's Austin Theatre Group premiered Frank Behringer's production December 3, 1975. This English version, translated by Helen Fehervary and Marc Silberman, was published with the German text in *New German Critique,* 8, Spring 1976. The first German publication appeared shortly after in the literary magazine *Alternative,* 110-111, 1976.

MAUSER is Müller's response to Bertolt Brecht's Lehrstück, *Die Massnahme (The Measures Taken,* in Eric Bentley's translation). Both plays investigate the failure of devoted revolutionaries and their acceptance of a death sentence pronounced by the party. Brecht's protagonist failed due to spontaneous empathy, compassion, and emotional involvement with the oppressed; one of Müller's protagonists fails due to a similar weakness, the other (whose name in an early version of the piece was Mauser) eventually embraces executions as an integral and even rewarding part of his revolutionary mission. He begins to kill for killing's sake and only by execution can he be stopped and further damage to the Revolution prevented, an execution he learns to willingly accept as his last service to the Revolution.

Brecht's text reflected on the fight of the German Left and its Communist Party against Hitler and Germany's rising Fascism; distancing his fable by way of an East Asian setting, he warned of pitfalls while pointing out possible strategies in this struggle. Müller's play represents a post-Stalin viewpoint. Using as well as criticizing the model Brecht created in *Die Massnahme,* and also quoting from other works by Brecht, such as *The Mother,* it reflects the author's experience and perception of Stalinism. When we go back to the short paragraph in A B C (written in the early fifties) that contained the core of Müller's fable, it is clear how long and how fervently the issues of MAUSER engaged his imagination. Looking at his most recent work, VOLOKOLAMSK HIGHWAY, one discovers that Müller has begun to reinvestigate these issues, and the form itself from which he had taken leave with MAUSER.

The text's title refers to the famous "Mauser" pistol, designed by the nineteenth-century German weapons manufacturers, the brothers Mauser. This handgun became a favorite with the Red Army during the Russian civil war. The poet Mayakovsky praised it in his "Left March" of 1918: "Silence, you orators! / You / Have the floor / Comrade Mauser."

The German word "Mauser" also denotes the change of feathers undergone by birds in Spring and Fall.

C. W.

Stefan Odry

MAUSER
Messepalast, Vienna, 1987.

CHORUS: You have fought at the front of the civil war
  The enemy hasn't found any weakness in you
  We haven't found any weakness in you.
  Now you yourself are a weakness
  The enemy must not find in us.
  You dispensed death in the city of Witebsk
  To the enemies of the Revolution by our order
  Knowing, the daily bread of the Revolution
  In the city of Witebsk as in other cities
  Is the death of its enemies, knowing, even the grass
  We must tear up so it will stay green
  We have killed them, using your hand.
  But one morning in the city of Witebsk
  You yourself have killed with your hand
  Not our enemies, not by our appointment
  And you must be killed, an enemy yourself.
  Do your work now at the last place
  The Revolution appointed you to
  The place you won't leave on your feet
  At the wall which will be your last one
  As you have done your other work
  Knowing, the daily bread of the Revolution
  In the city of Witebsk as in other cities

Is the death of its enemies, knowing, even the grass
We must tear it up so it will stay green.

A: I have done my work.

CHORUS: Do your last one.

A: I have killed for the Revolution.

CHORUS: Die for her.

A: I have committed a mistake.

CHORUS: You are the mistake.

A: I am a human being.

CHORUS: What is that.

A: I don't want to die.

CHORUS: We don't ask you if you want to die.
The wall at your back is the last wall
At your back. The Revolution doesn't need you any more.
It needs your death. But until you say Yes
To the No that has been pronounced on you
You haven't finished your work.
Facing the gun barrels of the Revolution which needs your death
Learn your last lesson. Your last lesson is:
You, who stand at the wall, are your own enemy and ours.

A: In prisons from Omsk to Odessa
On my skin the text was written
Once read under school benches and on the john
PROLETARIANS OF ALL COUNTRIES, UNITE
Written with fist and rifle butt, with boot heel and shoe cap
On the son of a middle class father who owned his own samovar
Prepared on floorboards which were hollowed from kneeling
Before the icon for a cleric's career.
But soon I left the starting point.
At meetings, demonstrations, strikes
Ridden down by orthodox cossacks
By sluggish officials listlessly tortured
I learned nothing of life after death.
Killing I learned in the everlasting combat
Against the mortal clinch, at the time of Die or Kill.
We said: He who won't kill won't eat.
To ram the bayonet into an enemy
Cadet, officer, or a peasant who hadn't understood anything
We said: It's work like any other work

To smash a skull or shoot.
A (CHORUS): But one morning in the city of Witebsk
    The noise of battle not far off, the Revolution gave me
    With the Party's voice the mandate
    To take charge of the Revolutionary Tribunal
    In the city of Witebsk, that dispenses death
    To the enemies of the Revolution in the city of Witebsk.
CHORUS: You have fought at the front of civil war
    The enemy hasn't found any weakness in you
    We haven't found any weakness in you.
    Leave the front and take the place
    The Revolution needs you at as of now
    Until it needs you at another place.
    Conduct our struggle in our back, dispense
    Death to the enemies of the Revolution.
A (CHORUS): And I agreed with the mandate.
    Knowing, the daily bread of the Revolution
    Is the death of its enemies, knowing, even the grass
    We must tear up so it will stay green
    I agreed with the mandate
    The Revolution had given me
    With the party's voice in the noise of battle./
    And this killing was another kind of killing
    And it was work unlike any other work.
CHORUS: Your work begins today. He who did it before you
    Must be killed before tomorrow, he himself an enemy.
A(CHORUS): Why he.
B: Before my revolver three farmers
    Enemies of the Revolution out of ignorance.
    On their backs the hands, tied by rope
    Are ruined by work, tied to the revolver
    By the Revolution's mandate is my hand
    My revolver aimed at their neck.
    Their enemies are my enemies, I know it
    But those standing before me, facing the quarry
    Don't know it, and I who know it
    Have no other lesson for their ignorance
    But the bullet. I have dispensed death
    The revolver my third hand

To the enemies of the Revolution in the city of Witebsk
Knowing, the daily bread of the Revolution
Is the death of its enemies, knowing, even the grass
We must tear up so it will stay green
Knowing, the Revolution kills with my hand.
I don't know it any more, I cannot kill anymore.
I retract my hand from the mandate
The Revolution gave me
One morning in the city of Witebsk
With the Party's voice, in the noise of battle.
I cut the rope at the hands
Of our enemies that are marked
With their work's trace as my own kind.
I say: Your enemies are our enemies.
I say: Go back to your work.
CHORUS (THE PERFORMERS OF THE THREE FARMERS):
And they went back to their work
Three enemies of the Revolution, uninstructed.
When he retracted his hand from the mandate
The Revolution had given him
One morning in the city of Witebsk
With the Party's voice, in the noise of battle
It was one hand more at our throat./
Namely, your hand isn't your hand
Just as my hand isn't my hand
Until the Revolution has finally triumphed
In the city of Witebsk as in other cities.
Namely, ignorance can kill
As steel can kill or fever
Since knowledge isn't enough, but ignorance
Must end once and for all, and it isn't enough to kill
But killing is a science
And must be learned, so it will end
Since what is natural isn't natural
But we must tear up the grass
And we must spit out the bread
Until the Revolution has finally triumphed
In the city of Witebsk as in other cities
So the grass will stay green and hunger will end.

He who insists on himself as his own property
Is an enemy of the Revolution like other enemies
Because our kind isn't our kind
And so aren't we, the Revolution itself
Isn't one with itself, but the enemy with
Tooth and nail, bayonet and machine gun
Writes into its living image his hideous features
And his wounds will be scars on our face.

B: Why the killing and why the dying
If the price of the Revolution is the Revolution
Those to be freed the price of freedom.

A: These or other words he shouted against the noise of battle
That had increased and still was increasing.
A thousand hands at our throat, there was
Against doubt in the Revolution no
Other remedy but the death of the doubter.
And I had no eyes for his hands
As he stood before my revolver, facing the quarry
If they were ruined by work or were not ruined
But they were tied firmly with rope
And we killed him with my hand
Knowing, the daily bread of the Revolution
Is the death of its enemies, knowing, even the grass
We must tear up, so it will stay green.
I knew it, killing others on another morning
And at a third morning others again
And they had no hands and no faces
But the eye I looked at them with
And the mouth I talked to them with
Was the revolver and my words the bullets
And I didn't forget it when they screamed
As my revolver hurled them into the quarry
Enemies of the Revolution to other enemies
And it was work like any other work.
I knew, if you shoot into a human being
Blood will flow from him as from all animals
Little differentiates the dead and
The little not for long. But man is no animal:
The seventh morning, I saw their faces

The hands on their back, tied with rope
Marked by the trace of their various work
While, facing the quarry, they waited
For death from my revolver, and doubt
Lodged itself between finger and trigger, burdening
With those killed over seven mornings
My neck which carries the yoke of the Revolution
So that all yokes will be broken
And my hand which is tied to the revolver
By mandate of the Revolution, given
One morning in the city of Witebsk
With the voice of the Party, in the noise of battle
To dispense death to its enemies
So the killing will end, and I spoke the command
This morning just as the first morning
DEATH TO THE ENEMIES OF THE REVOLUTION
And dispensed death, yet my voice
Spoke the command like it wasn't my voice and my hand
Dispensed death like it wasn't my hand
And the killing was a killing of another kind
And it was work like no other work
And at night I saw my face
That looked at me with eyes not my own
Out of the mirror, many times cracked
From the shelling of the city many times taken
And during the night I was not a man, burdened
With those killed over seven mornings
My sex the revolver that dispenses death
To the enemies of the Revolution, facing the quarry.
A (CHORUS): Why I. Relieve me of the mandate
    I am too weak for it.
CHORUS: Why you.
A: I have fought at the front of civil war
    The enemy hasn't found any weakness in me
    You haven't found any weakness in me
    Now I myself am a weakness
    The enemy must not find in us.
    I have dispensed death in the city of Witebsk
    To the enemies of the Revolution in the city of Witebsk

Knowing, the daily bread of the Revolution
Is the death of its enemies, knowing, even the grass
We must tear up, so it will stay green.
I did not forget it on the third morning
And not on the seventh. But on the tenth morning
I don't know it any more. To kill and to kill
And each third one, maybe, is not guilty who
Stands before my revolver, facing the quarry.
CHORUS: In this struggle that won't end
    In the city of Witebsk as in other cities
    But with our triumph or fall
    With two weak hands each one of us does
    The work of two thousand hands, broken hands
    Hands tied with chains and rope, hands
    Hacked off, hands at our throat.
    A thousand hands at our throat, we don't
    Have the breath left to ask for guilt or innocence
    Of each hand at our throat, or their extraction
    If they are ruined by work or are not ruined
    If misery twined them around our throat and
    Ignorance about their misery's root
    Or fear of the Revolution which will tear it up
    By its root. Who are you, different from us
    Or special, who insists on his weakness.
    He who says: I with your mouth, is not you.
    Not until the Revolution has finally triumphed
    In the city of Witebsk as in other cities
    You are your own property. With your hand
    The Revolution kills. With all the hands
    With which the Revolution kills, you kill too.
    Your weakness is our weakness
    Your conscience is the breach in your consciousness
    Which is a breach in our front. Who are you.
A: A soldier of the Revolution
CHORUS: So you want
    The Revolution to relieve you of the mandate
    You are too weak for, yet which needs to be achieved
    By some man or other.
A (CHORUS): No./And the killing continued, facing the quarry.

Next morning before my revolver a farmer
As before him his kind at other mornings
As before me my kind before other revolvers
Cold sweat at his neck: four fighters of the Revolution
Were betrayed by him to our enemy and his
Cold sweat at their neck, they stand before other revolvers.
His kind has been killed
And my kind, for two thousand years
By wheel gallows rope garrote knout katorga
By my enemy's kind who is his enemy
And my revolver aimed at his neck now
I wheel gallows rope garrote knout katorga
I before my revolver, facing the quarry
I my revolver aimed at my neck.
Knowing, with my hand the Revolution kills
Abolishing wheel gallows rope garrote knout katorga
And not knowing it, before my revolver a man
I between hand and revolver, finger and trigger
I breach in my consciousness, in our front.
CHORUS: Your mandate is not to kill men but
    Enemies. Namely, Man is unknown.
    We know that killing is work
    But Man is more than his work.
    Not until the Revolution has finally triumphed
    In the city of Witebsk as in other cities
    Will we know what that is, Man.
    Namely, he is our work, the unknown one
    Behind the masks, the one buried in the dung
    Of his history, the real one beneath the leprosy
    The living one in those petrifications
    Because the Revolution will tear off his masks, efface
    His leprosy, wash from the petrified dung
    Of his history his image, Man, with
    Teeth and nail, bayonet and machine gun
    Rising from the chain of generations
    Rending his bloody umbilical cord
    In the lightning of the real beginning, recognizing himself
    The one the other, according to their difference
    By the root, digs up Man from man.

What counts is the example, death means nothing.
A: But in the noise of battle that had increased
    And still was increasing, I stood with bloody hands
    Soldier and bayonet of the Revolution
    And asked with my own voice for assurance.
A (CHORUS): Will the killing end when the Revolution has triumphed
    Will the Revolution triumph. How much longer.
CHORUS: You know what we know, we know what you know
    The Revolution will triumph or Man will not be
    But disappear in the increasing mass of mankind.
A: And I heard my voice say
    This morning as at other mornings
    DEATH TO THE ENEMIES OF THE REVOLUTION and I
        saw
    Him who was I kill a thing of flesh blood
    And other matter, not asking for guilt or innocence
    Not for its name and if it was an enemy
    Or no enemy, and it stopped moving
    But he who was I didn't stop killing it.
    He said:/
CHORUS: I have thrown off my burden
    On my neck the dead don't trouble me any longer
    A man is something you shoot into
    Until Man will rise from the ruins of man./
    And after he had shot again and again
    Through the bursting skin into the bloody
    Flesh, at cracking bones, he voted
    With this feet against the corpse.
A (CHORUS): I take under my boot what I have killed
    I dance on my dead with stomping steps
    For me it isn't enough to kill what must die
    So the Revolution will triumph and the killing end
    But it shouldn't be here any more and be nothing forever
    And disappear from the face of the earth
    A clean slate for those who will come.
CHORUS: We heard his roaring and saw what he had done
    Not by our mandate, and he didn't stop screaming
    With the voice of Man who is devouring Man.
    Then we knew that his work had used him up

And his time had passed and we led him away
An enemy of the Revolution like other enemies
And not like others since also his own enemy
Knowing, the daily bread of the Revolution
Is the death of its enemies, knowing, even the grass
We must tear up so it will stay green.
But he had thrown off his burden
That was to be born until the Revolution has triumphed
On his neck the dead didn't trouble him any longer
They who will trouble us until the Revolution has triumphed
Since his burden had become his spoils
Hence the Revolution had no place for him any longer
And he had no place any longer for himself
Other than before the gun barrels of the Revolution.

A: Not until they took me away from my work
And took the revolver away from my hand
And my fingers were still crooked as around the weapon
Separate from me, did I see what I had done
And not until they led me away did I hear
Again my voice and the noise of battle
Which had increased and still was increasing.

A (CHORUS): But I am led to the wall now by my own kind
And I who understand it, do not understand it.
Why?

CHORUS: You know what we know, we know what you know.
Your work was bloody and like no other work
But it must be done like any other work
By some man or other.

A: I have done my work. Look at my hand.

CHORUS: We see that your hand is bloody.

A: How not so.
And louder than the battle noise the silence was
In the city of Witebsk for one moment
And longer than my life was this moment.
I am a man. Man is no machine.
Kill and kill, be the same after each death
I couldn't do it. Give me the sleep of machines.

CHORUS: Not until the Revolution has triumphed
In the city of Witebsk as in other cities

Will we know what that is: Man.

A: I want to know it here and now: I ask
   This morning in the city of Witebsk
   With bloody boots on my last walk
   He who is led to dying, who hasn't time left
   With my last breath here and now
   I ask the Revolution about Man.

CHORUS: You are asking too early. We cannot help you.
   And your question doesn't help the Revolution.
   Listen to the noise of battle.

A: I only have one time to live.
   On the other side of the battle noise like black snow
   Is waiting for me: silence.

CHORUS: You only die one death
   But the Revolution is dying many deaths.
   The Revolution has many times, not one
   Too many. Man is more than his work
   Or he won't exist. You don't exist any more
   Since your work has used you up
   You must disappear from the face of the earth.
   The blood you have stained your hand with
   When it was a hand of the Revolution
   Must be washed off by your own blood
   From the name of the Revolution which needs each hand
   But not your hand any longer.

A: I have killed
   By your mandate.

CHORUS: And not by our mandate.
   Between finger and trigger, the moment
   Was your time and ours. Between hand and revolver, the span
   Was your place at the front of the Revolution
   But when your hand became one with the revolver
   And you became one with your work
   And had lost any consciousness of it
   That it had to be done here and now
   So that it won't have to be done any more and by no one
   Your place at our front became a gap
   And no place for you at our front any longer.
   Terrible is what is custom, lethal what's easy

With many roots the past is dwelling in us
That is to be torn up with all its roots
In our weakness the dead are arising
Those to be buried, again and again
We have to give up ourselves, each one of us
But we shouldn't give up one another.
You are the one and you are the other
Whom you have mangled under your boot
Who has mangled you under your boot
You gave yourself up, the one the other
The Revolution won't give you up. Learn to die.
What you learn will increase our experience.
Die learning. Don't give up the Revolution.

A: I refuse. I won't accept my death.
My life belongs to me.

CHORUS: Nothingness is your property.

A (CHORUS): I don't want to die. I throw myself on the ground.
I hold on to the earth with all my hands.
I bite with my teeth into the earth to hold on
To what I don't want to leave. I scream.

CHORUS (A): We know that dying is work.
Your fear belongs to you.

A (CHORUS): What will come after death.

CHORUS (A): He still asked but got up from the ground
Not screaming any more, and we answered him:
You know what we know, we know what you know
And your question won't help the Revolution.
When life will be an answer
It might be permitted. But the Revolution needs
Your Yes to your death. And he didn't ask any more
But went to the wall and spoke the command
Knowing, the daily bread of the Revolution
Is the death of its enemies, knowing, even the grass
We must tear up so it will stay green.

A (CHORUS):
DEATH TO THE ENEMIES OF THE REVOLUTION.

Note

MAUSER, written in 1970 as the third piece of an experimental sequence, of which the first was PHILOKTETES, the second THE
HORATIAN, presupposes/criticizes Brecht's theory and practice of
the Learning Play. MAUSER, a variant of a theme from Sholo-
khov's novel *Quiet Flows the Don*, is not a play for the repertoire;
the extreme case is not the topic, but the example with which the
continuum of a normality that has to be exploded is demonstrated;
death—in the theatre of individuals tragedy was based on its
glorification, comedy on its inhibition—is shown as a function of life
that is regarded as production, one kind of work among others,
organized by the collective and organizing the collective. SO THAT
SOMETHING CAN ARRIVE SOMETHING HAS TO GO THE
FIRST SHAPE OF HOPE IS FEAR THE FIRST APPEARANCE
OF THE NEW IS TERROR. Performance for an audience is possible if the audience is invited to control the performance by its text,
and the text by its performance, through reading the Chorus part, or
the part of the First Player (A), or if the Chorus part is read by one
group of spectators and the part of the First Player by another group
of spectators—the text not read by each group should be blotted out
in the script—or through other devices; and if the audience's reac-
tion can be controled through the non-synchronism of text and performance, the non-identity of speaker and performer. The proposed
distribution of text is variable, the mode and degree of variants a
political choice that has to be made in each individual case. Examples of possible variants: The Chorus provides to the First Performer for certain speeches a performer of the First Performer (A 1);
all Chorus performers at once or one after another, perform the part
of the First Performer; the First Performer speaks certain segments
of the Chorus' speeches while A 1 performs his role. No performer
can assume another's role all the time. Experiences are only
transmitted by and in a collective; the training of the (individual)
capacity to make experiences is a function of the performance. The
Second Performer (B) is played by a member of the Chorus who,
after his killing, will again assume his place in the Chorus. All tools
of the theatre should be totally visible when employed: props,

costume pieces, masks, make-up utensils, etc., are on stage. The city of Witebsk is representative of all places where a revolution was is will be forced to kill its enemies.

H. M., 1970

THE BATTLE

Scenes from Germany

THE BATTLE (*Die Schlacht*) was written between 1951 and 1974. Müller began to formulate these "answers" to Brecht's collection of scenes about Nazi Germany, *Fear and Misery of the Third Reich*, in the early fifties, and he kept coming back to the material during the next two decades.

THE BEDSHEET was performed in 1974 at the Volksbühne in East Berlin, directed by Manfred Karge and Matthias Langhoff; a first printing of BEDSHEET had appeared eight years earlier in Sonderheft (Special Issue) 1, 1966, of *Sinn und Form,* the most prestigious East German literary magazine. Karge and Langhoff also staged at East Berlin's Volksbühne a first production of the complete play which opened October 10, 1975. The text was published in the *Programmheft* (Playbill) for the Volksbühne production, in *Jahresheft* (Yearbook) *1975*, of the West German theatre magazine, *Theater Heute,* and also in *Rotbuch* 134, 1975. An English translation by Marc Silberman, Helen Fehervary, and Guntram Weber was published in *Theater,* vol. XVII, 2, New Haven, 1986. The scenes received numerous productions in all four German-speaking countries, and also in many other languages.

The text clearly shows Müller's indebtedness to Brecht but also his doubts about Brecht's treatment of German fascism, against which he poses his own exploration motivated by, among other things, Artaud's writings and theatrical vision. However, he mainly drew upon his personal experience of the Nazi system and of World War II when, barely sixteen, he had been drafted into the paramilitary "Labor Service" during the last year of the war.

It would be wrong, though, to read this text simply as a "sick sheet" of the German nation during the twelve years of Hitler's rule. Müller confronts his reader/spectator with traits in the human unconscious, conditioned as it is by mankind's collective history, traits which keep nudging men towards behavior and actions that are perversely inhuman. One aspect all the scenes share is treason, another is a yearning for violence and killing that becomes overwhelming in moments of crisis or pressure.

These and other patterns of emotional responses or behavior which Müller depicts in THE BATTLE are, of course, not new to literature or the theatre. Yet, he aims at shaking his audience out of a complacency which makes it believe that such events as in THE BATTLE could only happen under an "inhuman" system, as Nazi rule was. They always can—and do—happen in a world where many advocate the survival of the fittest; a world "where a human history hasn't even begun," as Müller likes to point out.

While he presents a reading of the German mind between 1933 and 1945 that is drastically different from Brecht's interpretation, the author's language and dramaturgy are strictly formalized: his text also criticizes with its formal structures the realistic model Brecht had used.

C. W.

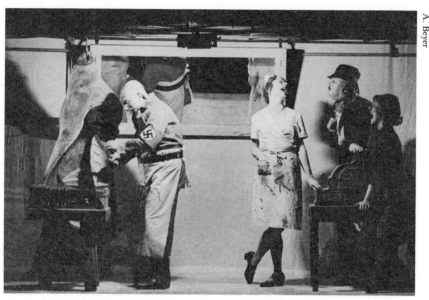

THE BATTLE
Volksbühne, East Berlin, 1975.
Directors: Wolfgang Karge / Matthias Langhoff.
Scene: Butcher and Wife.

Günter Schreckenberg

THE BATTLE
Staatstheater, Darmstadt, 1986. Director: Friedo Solter.
Scene: The Wedding.

THE NIGHT OF THE LONG KNIVES

A: And when the Reichstag burned, the night turned day
   In the door my brother stood, I looked away.
B: I am your brother.
A: Are you sure.
   And if you are, why are you coming here
   Before my face, your hands all red
   Of our comrades' blood. If three times you were dead.
B: That's what I want, brother, that's why I came.
A: You call me brother. I won't listen to that name.
   Between us there's a knife, they call it treason
   And it is you who forged it.
B: And if it's me and if my hand is red
   Give me what I ask for: To be dead.
A: Said my brother, no brother any longer
   But a disgrace and a mortal danger.
   Once, in their prisons, they had tortured him
   He wore a brownshirt now, ate from their plate.
   The wounds his hand afflicted were still fresh
   And now his gun was laying on my table.
   Do it yourself.

B: I'd have done it, if I could.
   I'm not the one I was.
A: What's that to me.
B: We are of the same mother.
A: Crawl back in.
B: I used to work next to you in the plant.
A: I wish the lathe had shredded you.
   What you became, I ought to have suspected.
B: During the general strike we were together.
   At Brandenburg gate in the roaring crowd
   I stood with you, the truth beneath my shirt.
A: Your shirt is brown, that is the truth today.
B: The truth today. You want to read it, brother.
   Three weeks long I have been the paper he
   Wrote his truth on, your enemy and mine.
   (Takes off the brownshirt. On his chest a swastika formed by
     fresh scars.)
   And what was left of him who was your brother
   Is the traitor.
A: What are you waiting for.
   Brother, do your job. And then look on
   While they torture me, and with good reason.
   Whatever, I won't play the dog for you.
B: Shall I tell you how a man is turned into a dog.
A: I see it on you: you have risen high.
   Crawl back into your skin, dog, the pack outside
   Is barking. Take your bite and share their spoils.
   (Pause. Noise of the city.)
B: I kept silent in the Gestapo basement.
   When I came out, the day didn't look brighter.
   You passed me like a stranger on the street
   My blood was not yet dry beneath the shirt.
   For you I took the beating, now I was
   Good for the garbage dump, and that was occupied.
   Round number two, after a three week break
   I almost felt at home down in the basement.
   Instead of handshakes there were kicking boots.
   When they went raiding, they took me along
   All spruced up. As if I'd been the snitch.

What is your worker's honor buying for you lately?
(*Dons the brown shirt.*)
I bought—where there's a dog there is a skin—
The brownshirt, carousels turn always right
And boots are great, you sure won't be alone
You swing the truncheon and the victims groan.
That's past. I looked deep down into myself.
The night of the long knives is asking who
Eats whom. I am the one and I'm the other.
There's one too many. Who'll cross out the other.
Take the revolver, do what I can't do
So I'm a dog no longer but a corpse.
A: While our comrades in the basements screamed
And long knives cut their swath across Berlin
I killed the traitor who's my brother, him.

I ONCE HAD A GOOD COMRADE

(*Four soldiers. Snow.*)

SOLDIER 1: Comrades, I can't see the enemy any more.
SOLDIER 2: That's hunger for you.
SOLDIER 3:   That's the snowdrifts.
SOLDIER 4: The enemy is everywhere.
SOLDIER 2:   My belly empty,
   I only know one enemy.
SOLDIER 4:   What do you try to tell us.
SOLDIER 2: The last four weeks I haven't seen a scrap of meat.
SOLDIER 3: A kingdom for a horse's bone.
SOLDIER 4: We starve for Germany.
SOLDIER 2:   What's that, Germany. Perhaps
   It's only the four of us now
SOLDIER 4:   One too many.
SOLDIER 2: (*Aiming at 4.*)   That's enough.
SOLDIER 4: I mean, we're comrades. And so it's . . .
SOLDIER 2: One is eating what the other shits.
SOLDIER 4: Better three bellies full than four empty
   Honor's marrow is called loyalty.

SOLDIER 3: (*Nods.*) One for all.
SOLDIER 2:   There's still a question: Who.

(*Soldiers 2, 3, 4 take aim at each other.*)

SOLDIER 1: Comrades, I can't hold my gun any longer.

(*Soldiers 2, 3, 4 put their guns down and look at each other. Pause.*)

SOLDIER 4:   Hand it over.
   I'll hold it for you, comrade.
   (*Takes the guns from him and shoots him.*)
                                   He was
   The weakest link and thus a jeopardy
   For our victory. And now as a good comrade
   He adds to our firepower.

(*Soldiers 2, 3, 4 eat 1. Song: "I ONCE HAD A GOOD COM-RADE."*)

A MIDDLE CLASS WEDDING

(*Man, wife, daughter. Hitler's picture.*)

MAN: Dear family, it's five to twelve
   It's time I help us quit this life
   We'll follow our Führer's great example
   The enemy'll be in our town tomorrow
   Who'd like to live in such a shame.
DAUGHTER: I do.
MAN: You'll take that back or I'll disown you.
   A German girl. I hardly can believe this.
DAUGHTER: Disown me, Daddy.
MAN: You'd like that, wouldn't you.
   This is no daughter of mine, now I'm sure.
   With whom did you betray me, woman.
WOMAN: Here on the spot I shall drop dead . . .
MAN: You shall, and in good time.
   (*To Daughter.*)
                                   And now for you:

You want to tell me something.

DAUGHTER: Yes.

Could I go to the toilet, Daddy.

MAN: You ought to control yourself, humans aren't animals.

Nobody is excused. Not with me.

What shall our brave foot soldiers say.

They are ready to give their life away.

It is the animal in you that's barking.

We must be tough. And that's the reason—

Wife, get the rope—I'll tie you now

To this chair.

(*Daughter bawls.*) Shut your trap and sit.

DAUGHTER: But, Daddy, if I have to . . .

MAN: We'll see to that.

(*To Wife.*)

We have to gag that person. Get me

A towel. Now let's get to work.

The Führer is dead, to live is treachery.

(*Puts the revolver to the daughter's temple, pulls the trigger.
There is no shot.*)

Damn it, I did forget to load it.

(*Loads gun and shoots daughter.*)

Good riddance.

WIFE: (*Screams.*) No.

MAN: Stop screaming.

Think of the Führer: better dead than red.

The best our life can offer is a hero's death.

You'll be there right away. I'm coming soon.

(*Shoots the wife, puts the gun to his temple, puts it down again,
looks into the muzzle, at the corpses, turns away, puts the gun
to his head again and puts it down again, etc. Hitler steps out
of the picture. Salute.*)

My Führer. It is he. My knees are failing me.

(*Hides the revolver from Hitler. Hitler wags his finger.*)

Where's my revolver. I know how to do it.

(*Turns the Hitler picture to the wall. Hitler disappears.*)

Where there was an end, there will be a beginning.

He who is strong is strongest when alone.

(*Exits.*)

BUTCHER AND WIFE

IN A BROWN SHIRT AND IN CLOVER

(Butcher shop in a small town. The man takes off his butcher's smock and dons the uniform of a Storm Trooper. The wife takes the smock and hands him the uniform pieces.)

WIFE: Since you joined the Storm Troopers, I won't have a minute's rest. They're lining up in the street for their seven ounces, and I can't be fast enough for anyone.

MAN: My joining the Storm Troopers was a customer service. We wouldn't have any meat on the hook. And your bed would be empty too, right. Better brown than army-gray.

WIFE: I won't complain.

MAN: *(Paints a swastika on his forehead, the wife is holding the mirror.)* An enemy bomber crashed close to town, in the woods at the river, an American.

WIFE: And you people are supposed to take him prisoner, aren't you.

MAN: What do I know.

STORM TROOPERS MARCHING

(German woods. Storm Troopers marching. Off-stage, the sounds of German fascism: Speeches   Heil shouts   Beerhall brawls   Crystal Night   War.)

STORM TROOPERS: Heinz has grown a lot / Till the very end at the machine gun / Siegfried looks more and more like me / The letter arrived yesterday / Three times operated it's the gall bladder / The Eastern front is looking pretty bad / Could you cough up something, my eldest girl is getting engaged / Till the very end at the machine gun / I can't do it / The letter arrived yesterday / Did you say the Eastern front is looking pretty bad / I'm drinking my beer, this broad comes in, a redhead / Maybe I can do it / But not a word to my wife / Did you hear this one: a Jew goes to the cathouse. Says the madam: You can't go up now, Goebbels is upstairs. Says the Jew / 'Toon Halt / He has had it / Rip his guts out / Off with his pumpkin / He's half charred/A

nigger maybe / Jews the lot of 'em (*Pause, while only the groans of the wounded pilot are to be heard.*)
GROUP LEADER: That's your line, Sabest, you're a butcher.

OF THE AMERICAN

(*Butcher shop. Butcher and Wife. Customers.*)

FEMALE CUSTOMER: My husband sends his congratulations, Mr. Sabest, for the Cross of Merit. Our Mr. Sabest, if he'd be at the front, he'd make chopped steak of the Russians. Three schnitzel.
CUSTOMER: The home front needs men, too, right, Mrs. Sabest.
WIFE: My husband is ailing. Or else he wouldn't be here any more. A cut of the pork?
MALE CUSTOMER: (*Laughs.*) Of the American.

BUTCHER'S DREAM

(The inside of an animal/human being. [A forest of entrails.] Blood raining. A dummy, larger than life and dressed in stars and stripes, hangs from a parachute. Storm Troopers in boar masks shoot at the dummy, first single shots, then all together. Sawdust trickles from the bullet holes. [The shots without a sound, viz. with a silencer.] As soon as the dummy's frame is empty, it is ripped off the parachute and torn to shreds. Dance of the boar masks. They trample the shreds into the sawdust.)

THE WIFE

'Twas April, night, the shooting wakes me up
And in the firing's glare I see the empty bed.
I know at once, he went the corpse's way
The American's, since the Russian's are coming.
I think maybe it's for the best, tomorrow
The Russians will be here, and better I
Will be a widow than the wife of someone
Who is living only for his execution.
Then I get up: without a man what am I?
Can't run the shop, and who'll be the butcher

Unloading meat, that is also a man's job.
There are the children, too. It's easy for
A man to drown himself when he sees no way out.
And here I am, three children to provide for
And lucky if there's not one in my belly
Who's helping me.

And in my nightshirt I ran after him
Down to the river, key in hand, house locked
And asked myself while running: Why do you run
Turn back Stop now Slow down What will be will be
You haven't done in that American
A volunteer or not, he was the killer
If you overtake him what's the gain
If you are too late what is the loss.
But as if they were not a part of me
My legs keep running on and on. And then
I hear him stumbling through the stubborn reeds
Towards the deep, the corpse is riding him.
I think: he cannot swim, that's good for him
He's dying easy. Then I hear him howl
While drowning.
What else could he have done but shoot that day.
The shop did business afterwards, most of the
Storm Troopers started buying meat from us
Blood's catching flies. But this is also true:
He need not be in such a hurry chasing
After a speedy death and turn me into
A widow since the Russians are coming.
That American, if he hadn't shot him
He had his orders, too, and war is war.
Who would have known it turned the other way
Before grass covered him, when victories
Were following each other without fail.
And now it turned that way and he is dying.
But that's the past. Why am I standing still
My hands stopping my legs from moving on
So I don't rush and go and drag him out.
He is my husband. That I'll die with him

Because I lived with him was not the deal.
I always have been a good wife to him
The shop, the housework, and the children too
And spread my legs whenever he did ask me.
How do I look now. Hands like graters and
My knees are calloused. That are the best years of
My life. To whom do I owe anything.
He cannot swim. I'll go and pull him out.
But if he takes me down with him, what will
Happen to the children.
Maybe if I pull him ashore I will
Only drag him to his execution. Why me.
Maybe it is too late now. All is quiet.
The shooting's coming closer. That's the Russians.
Better I know from nothing. Home before dawn.
The fish won't eat him. Husband mine.
If they find him, I don't know a thing.
Maybe it's not too late. I'll get him out

(Struggle in the water.)

Now I have killed him. It was him or me.
The water would have done the job without me.
And now it's me who showed the way to him.
Am I supposed to take it when a man
Rips off my head. There are the children, too.
Dead is dead.

THE BEDSHEET OR THE IMMACULATE CONCEPTION

(Berlin 1945. A basement. Two women on suitcases.)

A MAN: *(Enters.)*
    The Russians over there. Here, the SS.
    Across the street the butcher shop burned down.
    All those fine hams.
    (Battle noise.)
A SOLDIER: *(Comes rushing in, tears his uniform off.)*
                    Did you see anything?

(*Silence.*)

THE MAN: That smacks of treason.

THE SOLDIER: I need civvies now.

THE MAN: (*To the Young Woman.*)
  See if the Russians are closer.

(*The woman crawls upstairs. Silence. The woman returns.*)

YOUNG WOMAN: Yes.

(*The man tosses a jacket to the soldier.*)

THE MAN: A bedsheet.

OLD WOMAN: Not of mine.

YOUNG WOMAN: Have I got more?

THE SOLDIER: (*To the Old Woman.*)
  Your sheet won't warm you, woman, when you're cold.

OLD WOMAN: And the SS, when they see that hang outside
  They'll hang us.

THE MAN: That's true, too. There's no way out.

(*Battle noise.*)

THE SOLDIER: Whatever's coming closer isn't the SS.

THE MAN: Well, Comrade, you have learned what courage is.
  Show us what you have learned. Woman, the sheet.

(*The women hand over the bedsheets. The man hands one sheet on
to the soldier.*)

THE SOLDIER: I'll do what you want.

THE MAN: Yes. And do it fast.

(*The soldier exits with the sheet and returns with empty hands. Two
SS-men enter the basement, dragging the torn bedsheet behind them
on the floor.*)

1st SS-MAN: What do you see, comrade?

2nd SS-MAN: I see two traitors.

1st SS-MAN: (*Aims the machine gun at his comrade.*)
  Two?

2nd SS-MAN: Four.

1st SS-MAN: And what do traitors get?

2nd SS—MAN: (*Grins and pulls a rope from his pocket.*)
The rope.

THE MAN: Please, gentlemen, leave us out. It was him.
  (*He points at the soldier.*)

THE SOLDIER: (*Points at the man.*)
  I only did what he had asked for.

THE MAN: I
  Didn't ask him.

OLD WOMAN: We didn't ask a thing.

(*Battle noise. The SS-men jump the soldier and drag him out. The soldier screams.*)

YOUNG WOMAN: Hear him scream.

OLD WOMAN: No more.

THE MAN: I'll get the jacket.

(*The man crawls upstairs and returns quickly, without the jacket.*)

THE MAN: The Russians are coming. What is running
  Is the SS. They've taken off his jacket.

(*Two soldiers and a commander of the Red Army enter the basement, the soldiers carry the corpse of the deserter and put it on the shoot.*)

COMMANDER: Hitlerkaputtnowpeace. Son?

THE MAN: Son.

(*The old woman nods vigorously.*)

COMMANDER: Chleb.

(*One of the soldiers tosses her a loaf of bread, the other breaks his loaf across the knee and shares it with the first one. Commander and soldiers salute and leave the basement. Over the corpse the fight of the survivors for the bread begins.*)

1951/1974

Literature Must Offer Resistance to the Theatre

LITERATURE MUST OFFER RESISTANCE TO THE THEA-
TRE (*Literatur muss dem Theater Widerstand leisten*), a discourse
with Horst Laube, the dramaturg of the Frankfurt Schauspiel, was
first published as ''The Dramatist and the History of His Times'' in
Theater Heute, Yearbook 1975, Berlin, 1975. It was reprinted with
its present title in the volume *Gesammelte Irrtümer* (Collected Er-
rors), Frankfurt am Main, 1986.

This extended discussion with Horst Laube—not only the
Frankfurt Schauspiel's dramaturg, at the time, but also a playwright
whose *The Marathon Piano Player* (*Der Dauerklavierspieler*) had
premiered at Frankfurt in 1974—offered Heiner Müller the occasion to explain in detail the positions he held in 1975. It was the
year which saw the first stagings of THE BATTLE and MAUSER;
the latter in Austin, Texas, where Müller arrived as a visiting pro-
fessor in the Fall of 1975 for his first sojourn in America. Many of
the events, facts, and personalities to which Müller refers had
significance in the seventies; by now they are part of past history.

Of Müller's own writings referred to, THE CONSTRUCTION
SITE is a play describing conflicts and problems during the construction of a huge GDR industrial project in the fifties. It was written in 1963/64 and first published in the East German literary jour-
nal *Sinn und Form* 1/2, Berlin, 1965. Due to political objections
by the GDR's cultural authorities, the play had to wait fifteen years
for its first performance in 1980, at the Volksbühne, East Berlin.

CEMENT, an adaptation of Fjodor Gladkov's Soviet novel from
the twenties, was written for the Berliner Ensemble where Müller
was a playwright-in-residence and dramaturg in the early seventies.
It was premiered in 1973 at Brecht's former theatre, and published
in *Theater der Zeit* 6, East Berlin, 1974. The first performed example of Müller's efforts at the form he later called ''synthetic fragment,'' it contained shorter or extended pieces of narrative prose inserted into the frequently versified, but basically realistic dialogue of
the play. The prose pieces paraphrased stories from Homer's *Iliad*
and the ancient Prometheus and Heracles myths.

During his time with the Berliner Ensemble, Müller also worked as a dramaturg on Brecht's *Baden Learning Play*. His version of Brecht's FATZER fragment was first produced in Hamburg, and eventually by the Berliner Ensemble in the eighties, long after Müller had left the company.

The variant of *The Measures Taken* he mentions is, of course, his text MAUSER, premiered by a student theatre group at the University of Texas, Austin, half a year after his discussion with Laube.

Peter Palitzsch was Brecht's chief-dramaturg and also a director with the Berliner Ensemble. Since 1961, he has worked in the West and was at the time of this conversation one of the artistic directors of the Frankfurt Schauspiel where he staged Müller's CEMENT in 1975.

"Mitbestimmung"—a model of theatre administration characterized by the consensus all members of a company achieve in discussing each new project in minute detail, such as casting, concept, and so forth, was tried at several theatres in West Germany during the late sixties or early seventies. The most visible examples of this model were the Berliner Schaubühne and the Frankfurt Schauspiel. In spite of considerable artistic achievements, such experiments were eventually abandoned at the end of the seventies.

Peter Hacks, an acclaimed East German playwright, began his career during the fifties with such plays as *The Opening of the Indian Age* (a view of Columbus's discovery of America), and *The Battle of Lobositz* (an anti-war comedy, based on the rifleman Ulrich Braeker's memoirs of the Seven-Years-War, 1756-63). He also adapted Synge's play *Playboy of the Western World* for Brecht's Berliner Ensemble in 1955. Hacks eventually became one of the most performed contemporary playwrights in the four German-speaking countries; he was represented in New York with *Amphitryon* at Lincoln Center's Forum Theatre, in 1970, and with *Charlotte*, performed on Broadway in 1980 by Uta Hagen. Since the mid-sixties Hacks has worked towards a style which emulates European or German classic forms, in plays that include *Margaret in Aix, Prexaspes, Omphale,* and *Seneca's Death.* In his stage texts and in numerous essays, Hacks proposed a dramaturgical model which since has been labeled "Socialist Classicism." During the period of "Mitbestimmung," (democratic collective management), he argued against such experiments.

The West German playwright Martin Sperr is mainly known in America through his play *Hunting Scenes From Lower Bavaria*, which was presented at New York's Manhattan Theatre Club in 1981.

The social and artistic situation Müller describes in his concluding statement as typical for writers in the GDR has, of course, greatly changed during the last fourteen years, though many of his observations are still revelant.

C. W.

A DISCOURSE WITH HORST LAUBE ABOUT THE TEDIOUSNESS OF WELL-MADE PLAYS, AND ABOUT A NEW DRAMATURGY WHICH DELIBERATELY CHALLENGES THE SPECTATOR.

HORST LAUBE: *Drama is the story of great conflicts, anything else?*

HEINER MULLER: If, quite naively, I begin with the act of writing, I have a couple of times tried to write about myself and that always bored me very quickly, since it didn't seem important enough to me. That might be a mistake. On the other hand, it's also becoming ever more problematic for me to do something with so-called great characters who have a ''name.'' It does make a difference if someone is called Hamlet or Ham. Certainly, it's easier to work with characters when each of them has an immediate frame of reference. But it probably also blocks your creativity and narrows down the possible associations. If someone is called Ham, everything can happen that comes to mind in context with Hamlet but, then, you're still free of the constraints which the model exerts.

Would this imply that one must create characters who are so ''open'' that the spectators could slip into the character? With a Hamlet character, for instance, what he does is quite clearly described. But as a spectator one hardly has the chance to be inside this character. If you look at the kind of literature about presidents and generals which you find in Thomas Bernhard's work, what's happening up there on stage is at your disposal. You have an idea what such characters are like, and the the author introduces his own

*variant so that a general suprisingly behaves totally unlike a general.
That's a boring event.*

I think there is one interesting point. Especially since you talk of
Bernhard. I tried a couple of times to read plays by Bernhard, two I
have watched since they were shown on TV; *The Force of Habit*
and *The Hunting Party* I saw on stage in Vienna. I find it
remarkable how fast that bores me. I'm sure that it doesn't depend
on geographical or political conditions. He writes down what you
can accept as conversation when you're chatting, but written down
it's already boring. But I'm not sure I know precisely what the
reason is. These are things I wouldn't care to write down anymore.
That's also the problem between Beckett and Bond, for instance.
Bond writes down much more than what I could still write down.
Take *Lear* for instance. In his later plays self-pity begins, or a
philosophy of self-pity. Those are things you might think when you
have a bad time, but the moment you write them down they aren't
right anymore. I couldn't hold a pencil long enough to write that
down.

*Don't you think that there also is another ingredient in the work of
authors like Bond or Bernhard, that you always discover immediately a specific style the characters move within? Once the first lid of
style snaps shut, the play is in the can.*

That surely is the pressure of the market.

*Beckett doesn't have a style in that sense of the term. That his work
can be applied to all situations is proof of his openness, since his
work can't be seen any more as a reference to some event that just
happened, but it produces a "real" reality that by itself is true and
concrete. An author such as Bond always needs a reference to
something: Ah, this means that, this now stands for . . . while all efforts to claim Beckett wrote about human beings after the nuclear
holocaust soon were revealed as quite ludicrous. But then also the
question of dramatic conflict probably can't be asked any more in
this way—that one has to reproduce reality.*

If Realism is a useful term—in its application to the theatre—it
hasn't been questioned enough at all. Realism on the stage is, of
course, something quite different from realism in film or even in the
novel. It is, after all, totally unrealistic that people step unto a stage

and do something there while others are sitting and facing them. It certainly is an important aspect of Beckett's work that this is the foundation of his dramaturgy: the strangeness of the fact that people on a stage play something for other people who sit and watch it.

The first line in Endgame *is: "Well, now I play."*

The question is: to what degree is what's interesting in Beckett's work tied to a specific state of society or to an interpretation of this state which doesn't acknowledge history any longer and doesn't think of history anymore, where only situations exist and no history.

Don't you think this is realistic insofar as the feeling of a loss of history, or of an arrested, petrified history where nothing real happens anymore, has become a specific feeling among the middle classes, and that this feeling has found its most concrete expression in Beckett's work?

That's evident, I mean: that's Marxist, we don't have to tell this to each other. The problem is to discover why it has its impact even with the Marxists, for example with me. And why, for instance, even Brecht was interested in Beckett. Certainly with a counter-proposal in mind. But there is very little evidence of what Brecht's counter-proposal would have looked like, if he had directed a Beckett play.

Was that once a project of his?

There was a plan to produce *Godot*; it was probably one of Brecht's last projects. Hecht has published something on it, notes by Brecht and even a few efforts to place small social accentuations in the text which, however, weren't very successful. I know from conversations that Brecht wanted to contrast the game the characters play with each other in *Godot* with a film showing the historical process from World War II up to the Chinese Revolution. Obviously, as a beginning, a very sweeping general way to deal with it. But that doesn't mean much, it was a first try in approaching the project, and one can't know what would have come of it.

What do you think it is that interests you in Beckett? Isn't it true that sometimes one all too quickly analyzes characters in plays according to what is sociologically "tangible," and once that's been added up, they become nothing else but that? In Beckett's work

*there is a certain sediment of history, also caused by history that hap-
pened before someone's birth, that is a residue.*

When I worked on Brecht's *Baden Learning Play* with the Berliner
Ensemble, I found it interesting that it presented a kind of basic pat-
tern of several problems which Brecht later treated in different varia-
tions. The piece also contains nearly all of Beckett. But not only
that, there also is the problem of getting old, of dying, in the relation
between History and individual history. And that, of course,
becomes increasingly important in times when immediate actions
aren't the issue any more, when the revolution has to bide its time
or needs time, when one no longer has the option to walk into the
street and shoot or be shot. One simply has to work, and everything
takes a long time, and one doesn't know how long it will take, and it
can take longer than one's lifetime. Then the problem of the individual's aging or dying is of interest again.

*It makes much sense, however, that in times when history seems to
take slower steps you gain time to reassess. What, then, could the
theatre still learn? Watching performances you very rarely arrive at
the conclusion that you're seeing an option which inspires you also
as a writer. Yet, I'm also of the opinion that indeed only congenital
blindness or intentional blindness could somehow make wider this
suit which has become much too tight.*

When I'm writing a play and in doubt which stage direction I should
add, if this guy should walk on his hands or stand on his head or
crawl on all fours, I know—when that becomes a decisive question—that something is wrong with the text. As long as the text is
right, it is of no interest to me, it is a problem of the theatre or of
the director, if the character stands on his head or on his hands.
Whenever that becomes a problem for me, I haven't written
something in the right way. I firmly believe that literature has the
task of offering resistance to the theatre. Only when a text cannot be
done the way the theatre is conditioned to do it, is the text produc-
tive for the theatre, or of any interest.

*Because only if it offers resistance, can it change the theatre—and
the theatre change the text.*

There are enough plays which serve the theatre the way the theatre
is. One doesn't need to do that anew, it would be parasitic.

I see in your play CEMENT, *a new possibility of performance. One shouldn't look at the various layers of this piece vertically, but horizontally. That is, in a linear way and not separate them into especially valid ones, abstract ones, and then somewhat more realistic and, finally, fully realistic ones. One needs to investigate the effect of these various layers on the same level, in contradiction or in connection with each other.*

In CEMENT, in a scene between Kleist and Tchumalov, there are these two "commentary-texts"—the Homer piece and the Prometheus story. When I wrote the scene, I felt the need to insert these texts. Among other reasons, probably because I became bored after a while doing this dialogue between the two characters since I knew the course of it beforehand. It is determined by history and certainly also by my political presuppositions. On the other hand, the two characters aren't able to formulate what their historical function is and which game they are playing. From this derives the moral obligation for the author himself to speak to the issue. Tchumalov, for instance, doesn't know who Achilles is, he cannot know it according to his biography. I know it, Kleist knows it, too, consequently I have to help Tchumalov and somehow structure it into the scene. That's one aspect. But when I saw it acted, and also when I read it after it was completed, I suddenly had the very bad feeling that these commentary-texts were purely illustrative, that the scene was already stating this and that the texts were mere appendages. I believe a dangerous problem of the play is situated there. If you don't already assume the author's attitude—which led to those inserted texts—towards the dialogue sections, or establish such an attitude there, then the prose texts turn into appendages, into illustrations. You have to mould scenes in a way that such texts are to be waited for.

Another aspect of what you said about the slowing down of history's movement is, though, that on the other hand it's greatly accelerated. It's getting slower for the individual, in Europe, for us perhaps, subjectively. But objectively it's moving ever faster, and there is less and less time to intervene, to change something. This also leads to a situation where no time is left any more for a discursive dramaturgy, for a calm presentation of the state of affairs. Already when you begin to tell a story, you're thrown into a process which is moving faster than you could tell it in your story, and so by necessity its realization in relation to your model is off balance. Off balance is meant in a positive sense.

While you are implementing your plan, history has already over-taken you. When you talk of such objective acceleration, do you also mean that the degree to which reality is known has greatly increas-ed, that one can't afford to waste time any more but is ever more strongly forced to achieve the pace of this objective acceleration by the production of something not yet known?

First of all, if we start with Brecht for example, the problems have become everywhere much more conrete. The programs which to him still were designs, have meanwhile more or less entered a phase of concreteness, for better or worse, and that, too, exerts a remarkable pressure. I've written a play which, by virtue of its theme, is a variant of *The Measures Taken*, or a continuation. It hasn't yet been performed or printed but that will happen. Writing it, I noticed, (it's the form of the *Lehrstück,* if you like, but already a very much changed form of the *Lehrstück,* not simply presenting [the facts] but done in a way that it could only work if the people were sucked into the process from the beginning) that it was im-possible for me to use the term ''The Classics.'' For instance: ''The Classics said.'' That simply won't work anymore because in the meantime the Classics have no longer only spoken, but experiments now exist to concretely realize their designs. Such proverbial phrases don't work any more, you have to make everything concrete if it is to become visible at all.

To go back once more to CEMENT, *such concretizing can only work, after all, if the Prometheus story is not simply a classic by itself but if the Kleist-Tchumalov story produces the Prometheus story. Isn't there a danger—that seemed to happen when I saw the play's performance at the Berliner Ensemble—that one experiences various examples from recent or remote history, and the author is merely the representative of the problem? Isn't the issue rather if the engagement of the author and his desire to express himself or his message, or whatever, becomes so clearly recognizable that he couldn't express himself in any other way than in those examples? Where actually is the ''hole'' in such a play where you yourself ap-pear? I don't mean now your self-pity or your delights. Where do you appear as an example in the story?*

When I'm writing, I always have merely the desire to burden the recipients with so much that they don't know which should be the first item to carry, and I believe that is the only option. The question is how do you achieve this in the theatre. That not one thing is shown after another, which for Brecht was still a law. Today, one has to show as many points as possible at the same time so that people are forced to select. That is, they even may not be able to select any more, but have to decide quickly what they'd take on as their first burden. And it can no longer be done in such a way that you offer them information and say: But there is still that one, too. I believe the only way left to do it is by way of inundation. And I think it becomes rather boring if you separate those prose texts from the scenes, since then the spectators always have time to calm down. You must always pull one thing into the other if both are to attain their effect.

Perhaps we shouldn't give a hoot for a dramaturgy as long as it's creating harmony.

You can quote Brecht here. He once was asked, by Palitzsch I believe, if the production he directed—it was *The Caucasian Chalk Circle*, or maybe *Mother Courage*—wasn't already Epic Theatre. Brecht said Epic Theatre wasn't possible yet, it wasn't possible until the perversity of making a trade out of a luxury ended—the constitution of theatre by separation of stage and auditorium. Only when that is abolished—at least as a tendency—will it be possible to make theatre with a minimum of dramaturgy, that is nearly without dramaturgy. And that's the issue today: To create a theatre without effort. When I go to the theatre, I notice that I become ever more bored with watching one single train of action. That doesn't exactly interest me any longer. If in the first act an action starts, and in the second act a quite different one continues, and then a third and a fourth action begin, then its entertaining, pleasurable, but not the well-made play anymore.

That's why I think a billiard ball dramaturgy comes in very handy. A billiard ball rolls, collides with the next one, transfers its movement and stops. At the end you remember a system of billiard balls, a certain order which was the order of their movements.

Yes, the problem with the well-made play and with the train of action during one evening—I believe this has something to do with the changed starting point of authors. A well-made play, according to the prevailing criteria, is after all a product of manufacturing. I noticed years ago actually, that when I write I begin to sketch a scene and arrive at the moment when the hero could have his aria, and the first two lines come very easily, then I know how the aria is going to continue. Then I always feel the desire to hand this now to a workshop, with some instructions, a manual, since what I already know only bores and exhausts me. I believe it's indeed a problem that the theatre has accepted or applied far too few of the new technologies, from the fine arts, let's say. That, for instance, the collage has never really been applied as a method by the theatre.

Is that of interest?

I believe there is a contradiction in our audience between their interest and their needs. What interests people is what they don't need, and what they need doesn't interest them. One really has to search for ways to do what they need, even though they reject it. What they actually want in the theatre they relish the least. Just as there is a difference in the theatre between success and impact. That's a law, I believe. And if they are becoming congruent, it's the symptom of a crisis. We don't have to talk about it, it's a general phenomenon that bad plays or productions attract more audiences than good ones. You simply need the nerve to live with it and wait until it has exhausted itself.

So you believe that a playwright who depicts a clearly positive world wouldn't satisfy the needs—at most the interest—of our audiences?

He surely satisfies needs but these are very superficial needs. I don't believe that people go to the cinema for this kind of affirmation. In the cinema, they look for a broken world and in the theatre, they look for a whole world. That is a phenomenon which has grown with history, especially in Germany, since theatre always has been a matter of [social] representation and education.

Because it always had a surrogate function, and then the bourgeoisie put it in place of the church, in the same function—as an apparatus for the solution of ultimate questions and for the production of a harmony which in daily business life one was perfectly free to destroy.

The theatre, at least our theatre, still exists totally in this situation and it is forced to remain there. Consequently politics is not permitted to the theatre, the theatre is permitted only to deal with a specific segment of the world. It's proclaimed incompetent in every other respect.

You were just now a guest at a theatre, here at the Frankfurt Schauspiel, where your play CEMENT *will be produced and where also "Mitbestimmung" [a democratic model of collective management] is tried out. Well, generally speaking . . .*

There is nothing wrong with it, in my opinion!

. . . generally speaking, one tries "the regeneration of the theatre based on the actor," as Peter Hacks recently put it. Do you experience any anxiety having your play produced at such a theatre, where exhaustive efforts are made to let the contribution of everyone—that is: the productivity of everyone involved in the project—appear in the final result? I see I've already put this in a positive fashion . . .

I think the people who work hardest in the theatre are the actors. It would be simply asocial to deny them the right of participating in decisions. Hacks is a monarchist.

And what are you?

I wouldn't be able to define myself in such categories since I don't understand myself as a class.

By the way, what became of the so-called New Classicism? What of the theory according to which the fully achieved work of art is capable of anticipating in its form the solution of conflicts unresolved in reality as yet? During a certain period plays by you and by Peter Hacks were viewed according to this theory. The theory justified their immense perfection which was astounding but also a bit intimidating. One more question: Doesn't this theory contradict your partiality for the fragment and the fragmentary which you've stated just now?

The theory certainly is moronic, an especially refined kind of escapism. A classic literature is, first of all, the literature of a class. And if you absolutely want to talk about verse, *Tales From Landshut* by Martin Sperr, for instance, if you'd like to, you could say the play

covers somewhat similar problems here [in the FRG], as THE CON-
STRUCTION SITE does for my country. Yet, it's quite inconceivable that the people in Sperr's play speak in verse to each
other. As for THE CONSTRUCTION SITE, I think that it appears
relatively natural there, that it doesn't seem particularly artificial.
It's certainly caused by the fact that workers in my country have a
different comprehension of themselves and self-confidence versus
state authority or management, even when they express it negative-
ly or polemically. The fact is that a worker with us can talk much
more rudely or directly to his superior, his plant manager or party
secretary, than a worker here could afford to when talking to his
supervisor. Even if you regard it as a mere phrase that the working
class is the ruling class, it still has its effect: the phrase is a reality. A
worker with us is irreplaceable, here he is replaceable, a matter of
supply. That's an essential point, and it is actually much more a
prerequisite for versified speech than what Hacks had in mind.

For Hacks, the problem was, and still is, that he isn't quite of this
world. The GDR always was a fairytale to him—he experienced and
described her as a fairytale world. The trouble is that his theories,
because they are put so wittily and pointedly, always contain only a
half-truth. If they were right, it wouldn't sound so witty. That's
what creates the effect, since it's all so easily quotable. And for this
reason it became here [in the West] an abstract for the reading of
GDR drama, very regrettably so.

In our [Frankfurt] theatre, we are currently talking about Chekhov's
Seagull *and about authors as characters, as they appear in Chekhov's
work and also in Gorky's, in* Summerfolk *for instance. These writers
appear on stage chiefly as people who have forgotten how to write,
due to conditions which remain hidden in the cloud of an inscrutable
life. They are mostly played as liars and phonies. I think it's more
correct to see them as authors who can't write any more because
reality is no longer the way they need it. Is writing possible at all
when reality is moving ever more slowly, or when it's difficult to
recognize any movement at all?*

If you have written for a while, you yourself become a reality and
somehow you have to assume an attitude toward this reality. If you
have the impression or if it's objectively true that the movement is
slowing down, you have to extend your reach. And when I look at

our situation, it's probably more important at this time to reprocess Shakespeare's work than Brecht's. Shakespeare as a prerequisite for [reviving] Brecht—that is, much more than merely a prerequisite. You can see Brecht anew only after you've found a new entry to, a fresh way of dealing with, Shakespeare. And you acquire a new view of Brecht only if you stage new plays which in some way are determined by the fact that Brecht has worked and written in the GDR. But little is to be gained if you concentrate all your efforts exclusively on Brecht.

Do you have, then, a conception of what this new view of Brecht would look like? Is there already a possibility to develop such a new view? Or do you think that first an extended pursuit of other things is required?

One probably needs to investigate how much of Brecht hasn't been accepted as yet. And that is generally what is interesting in the history of German theatre and letters. The beginnings, the projects which weren't completed, which couldn't achieve an impact. In Kleist's work, certainly *Robert Guiskard* is highly interesting in this respect, and so is *Woyzeck* and the plays of Lenz. But everything that did receive recognition—I don't mean impact now—is antiquated and is sitting on bookshelves. Brecht is also on the bookshelves, to be sure, but very much of his writing hasn't even been noticed yet. Now, as far as I am concerned, the most important works of Brecht are the *Lehrstücke* and a few fragments. It also seems to me that the early plays are now more interesting than the so-called classic ones. If, for instance, one has staged *In the Jungle of Cities* or *Baal*, and immediately afterwards audiences see *Mother Courage* or *Galileo*, they see it in a different way than without knowing *In the Jungle*.

Just now you've mentioned fragments by Brecht, or fragments by other authors. You don't mean only fragments have a special literary value? You also see the fragmentary as a special value, don't you?

By all means. I generally believe that now the focus in the theatre should be directed more at the process than at results. That certainly is much more difficult here where you're more directly dependent on selling your stuff. That requires packaging, and a fragment doesn't come packaged. That's why I hope it will be easier to do this in my country. For instance, I think it's extremely interesting to explore the *Fatzer* material by Brecht. When you're here in the FRG, or when you work here, you can't help but recognize that the problems of Baader-Meinhof and the Anarchists are a most important theme. I believe that all the things literature is able to do with it, the level where the theme is interesting for the theatre, that all of it has been sketched in the *Fatzer* fragment.

You know the story: Four or five soldiers desert from the Western front [during World War II], since they believe the war will soon be over and the revolution will arrive. They hide in the apartment of one of them in Mülheim, in the Ruhr, and wait for the revolution. But the revolution is a long time coming. And so they destroy each other. I think this is a grand design that encompasses much of what is happening here and now. Responses to a development which you cannot accelerate or correct without broad-based support of the masses. The specific conditions of the Baader-Meinhof problem are also relevant for my country since conditions are, of course, much more difficult if a revolution merely takes place in the workaday routine. It becomes very difficult, then, not to become depressed, especially for intellectuals. An intellectual, after all, always needs a bit of theatre, a bit of glamor. And as long as that's provided, everything is fine. But when the issue turns out to be the enforcement of sanitary rules at the work place, which is for most people much more important than the concerns of the intellectuals, then it becomes a problem for intellectuals to stick by the cause.

Do you think that the intellectual also needs a certain theatricalization of reality?

It's hard for him to hold on to reality without getting bored. This certainly is also due to the fact that the intellectual enjoys a privileged position in the first place, also in my country. Certainly much more so than here.

That surely is because the intellectuals in the GDR, including the playwrights, have already described all those problems.

What problems are you talking about?

The revolution in everyday life or the revolution turning into a daily routine.

Probably more in a negative way, or starting with the negation, if I take myself as an example. Close to the end of THE CONSTRUC-TION SITE, a poet enters who is looking for those enormous conflicts: During Stalin's rule there must have been victims. Then he simply can't find such true victims and it's pointed out to him that a violation of sanitary rules is merely a violation of sanitary rules and not a motif for poetry, because it has become an administrative issue, a question of organization, which no longer needs the enormous expenditure of literature or the theatre. One simply has to take the necessary measures or change something. Then there won't be any victims killed and you will no longer need a literature that needs victims.

Once you look into your own head, how do you avoid the suspicion, since the revolution has become an everyday matter, that you create for yourself fictitious problems which enable you again to produce literature? Because the first word forces you to write the second, the third, and the fourth, until the day you die?

That's a problem I haven't resolved yet. Well, you talk of fictitious problems. If here someone commits suicide, it's quite normal, it doesn't pose a problem. Such things happen, that's life. Some can endure it and others can't and they, then, kill themselves. If in my country people kill themselves, it is an enormous problem for us since you don't quite expect that. Because, first of all, there are by far fewer objective reasons to commit suicide. There is no existential fear, no problem to find a job, all that doesn't exist. Consequently, one has to consider reasons and areas or dimensions which appear in our literature much too rarely. In this context, a story comes to mind that Sartre once quoted in some interview. A Soviet writer told him: When Communism has triumphed and all social and economic problems are resolved, the tragedy of Man begins. And that kind of tragedy exists here [in the West] only in its comedic diguise by Beckett. In the work of all the others it's far below the level of Beckett. But in my country it's a tragic issue. It simply shouldn't be necessary that human beings die. In this respect, I believe the field is very large and you don't have to resign yourself to fictitious problems for a long time to come. It's rather the way that we, including me, probably haven't explored enough the field of potential problems and conflicts.

Isn't this problem also representative of others which certainly don't appear very often in GDR literature?

Yes, because it's a much greater provocation in my country, of course, than here. Primarily it is a positive fact that the provocation is greater. But it also makes it more difficult to deal with it. That's also a reason I'm not afraid you won't find real problems any more and have to invent fictitious ones. The other side of the coin is that the problem of how a family might acquire a car is absolutely unfit for literature. It would never interest me and it's quite insignificant, even though cars are more expensive in the GDR. Here this could by all means become the topic of a play. For instance Kroetz, and that's perfectly alright the way he does it . . . But I don't believe it's relevant in my country. Even if you have to save for two years or more to buy a car, it's not a real problem because it's pretty much predictable when you'll have enough money to buy it, as long as you limit your expenditures in certain ways. That's why a lot of subjects simply aren't available, they aren't suitable any more for literature, they've been taken from our hands by social measures.

A complaint one hears very often against your plays is: They are certainly great works of art, of poetic language, but they are too indirect, obscured by mythological examples. One has to approach the plays' true mainspring by many roundabout trains of thought.

That certainly has somewhat to do with the historical situation of Socialism, also of the GDR, that everything is much more mediated. Beginning with the moment when the Russian revolution—which was actually made with the hope that a Western European, especially a German, revolution would follow—remained isolated, it existed in a most complex field of international complications and problems. Then, there isn't any simple step available any more; with each step so much has to be considered, so much left behind, so much carried along. I believe there is a starting point where simply much more has to be moved if a step forward is to be taken at all. Where much more is attached to it and also much more depends on it: a greater responsibility. That's already an aesthetics, and from it stems to a degree this effect of something translated and mediated that isn't easily accessible.

Don't you think that the role of the intellectual, of the writer in the GDR, could be an isolated one which has its own brand of ritual?

I'm quite sure that this is an honest answer: I've never pondered how to disguise something, that never was a problem for me. I believe I have never suppressed anything which came to mind. When I explored a topic, I wrote down everything I thought of in the context. It certainly has also to do with the fact that the intellectual's role in my country is somewhat questionable. In a certain way private property is also rescinded in the arts, of course.

I'm still concerned with the question: Where does the author's existence appear in his products? An observation by Roland Barthes much impressed me when he stated, more or less, that the truth of a work of art can only be communicated now if the author has invested all of his existence in it. Only then does it become an event in history, by way of telling us the history of the author.

In my country another aspect has to be added, of course. Since art isn't the kind of merchandise, after all, which it is here, first of all there comes into being—maybe also much more than here—a bad conscience among those who produce art. There is an otherwise not very important poem by a GDR poet: "I sit here and search for a rhyme"—I don't recall it literally now—"and I notice across the street—it's about five in the morning—smoke rising from the smokestack, they've already begun to work and they work so that I'm able to search for my rhyme." That is a quite mendacious expression of an important fact. What has been concealed here is the bad conscience you experience when you've spent half the night in search of a rhyme, or whatever, and then you see that people have worked day and night, for more or less than a rhyme. I believe you're much less able to ignore this fact in my country than here, and this condition plays its role when you're writing. It would, of course, be quite a defeatist consequence if you tried to shorten your search for the rhyme. Or if you began to feel that it isn't important if the rhyme is good or not, or if a text is correct or not. That would be criminal. It's also immoral, but you have to be aware that it's a privilege to be able to do work that you enjoy while the majority of the population has to work in a way which is absolutely impossible to enjoy in the long run, work that's done so others can enjoy theirs. And in my country you live with this contradiction much more than here when you write, I believe, since it isn't an issue here.

But I think it is also valid in reverse, of course. The man who works across the street also wants to enjoy the person who is writing. And that can't only remain a static relationship. It has to inspire both sides.

That is a question which can't be answered during my lifetime.

1975

TELEVISION

TELEVISION (*Fernsehen*) is a set of poems Müller wrote in the fall of 1989, reflections on the stunning images of recent history. This volume of his texts was about to go to press in early November just at the moment the Berlin Wall opened up, and the East German government resigned. Müller was in New York for three days to appear at The Kitchen in the music-theatre piece "The Man in the Elevator" (a section from his play THE TASK). He was asked by the publishers of PAJ if he wished to add any comment on the historic changes in East Germany to THE BATTLE volume. Müller offered these poems.

The first poem, of course, deals with the events of June 1989 in Beijing. "The monument of the dead Indians" is Müller's metaphor for the Statue of Liberty. The second juxtaposes Janos Kadar, himself a former victim of Stalinist show trials, who ruled Hungary for thirty-three years, and Imre Nagy, whose government was in power when Kadar called in the Russian army in 1956 to depose it. In 1989, the then deposed Kadar died, and the executed body of Nagy was exhumed to be given a state funeral. The line in capital letters is a quote from Brecht's poem "To Those Born After Us" (*An die Nachgeborenen*); the sentence continues: ". . . we couldn't be kind ourselves." In the third poem, the author quite obviously refers to several texts published in this volume.

C. W.

1   GEOGRAPHY

Across from the GREAT HALL OF THE PEOPLE
The monument of the dead Indians
On the SQUARE OF HEAVENLY PEACE
The track of tanks.

2   DAILY NEWS* AFTER BRECHT 1989

The torn-off fingernails of Janos Kadar
Who called in the tanks against his own people when they began
To string up his Comrades and torturers by their heels
His dying when the betrayed Imre Nagy
Was dug up again or what's left of him
BONES AND SHOES* The television was there
Secretly buried face down to the earth 1956
WE WHO WANTED TO PREPARE THE GROUND FOR
   KINDNESS
How much earth shall we have to eat
That tastes of our victims' blood
On the way to a better future
Or to none if we spit it out.

---

*English in the German original.

3   SELFCRITIQUE

My editors rummage through the old texts
Sometimes when I read them I shudder That's
What I wrote OWNING THE TRUTH
Sixty years before my presumable death.
On the tube I see my compatriots
With hands and feet vote against the truth
That forty years ago was my own.
What grave will protect me from my youth?